FAMILIES IN RECOVERY

FAMILIES IN RECOVERY

Working Together to Heal the Damage of Childhood Sexual Abuse

BEVERLY ENGEL

94

LOWELL HOUSE
LOS ANGELES
CONTEMPORARY BOOKS
CHICAGO

Engel, Beverly.
    Families in Recovery : working together to heal the damage of childhood sexual
abuse / Beverly Engel.
    p. cm.
    ISBN 1-56565-113-8
    1. Adult child sexual abuse victims—Family relationships.
    2. Adult child sexual abuse victims—Rehabilitation. I. Title.
RC569.5.A28E529 1994
616.85'822390651—dc20   93–48444
                                                                               CIP

Requests for such permissions should be addressed to:
Lowell House
2029 Century Park East, Suite 3290
Los Angeles, CA 90067

Publisher: Jack Artenstein
Vice-President/Editor-in-Chief: Janice Gallagher

This book is dedicated to my deceased mother, Olga Engel, in appreciation for her courage and willingness to grow and change, and to all the parents of survivors who are willing to believe their adult children and work with them toward healing.

CONTENTS

PART III
BRINGING THE FAMILY BACK TOGETHER

YOUR HEALING JOURNEY

To Survivors

If you were sexually abused as a child, you not only have the problems associated with your victimization to cope with but also the problem of resolving your issues with your family of origin. Whether you have already told members of your family about your sexual abuse or are planning to do so, this book will help maximize the possibility of your receiving what you so desperately need and desire—namely, to be listened to, believed, and understood.

If you have not told your family, *Families in Recovery* will guide you step-by-step through the process, helping you break the news to them in ways that will make it easier for them to hear it and that will facilitate communication. If you have already told your family but were not believed or were not given the kind of understanding and support you need, this book will help you make another attempt and possibly achieve better results this time.

We have all come a long way since childhood sexual abuse first became a national issue around the time of the McMartin Preschool case in 1984. When this and other cases hit the headlines, America began to take childhood sexual abuse seriously for the first time. Armed with the heady feelings of righteousness and political activism, many survivors began confronting their parents and families about the fact that they had been sexually abused. Because the secret of childhood sexual abuse had been kept hidden for so long, those who were finally being listened to and believed by therapists, women's rights advocates, and fellow survivors felt compelled to bring their secrets out of the darkness with a flourish. Their long-repressed anger came tumbling out in a torrent as they confronted first their parents and then their perpetrators.

Looking back on those days, I realize that I, like so many other therapists, may have been too one-sided in my admonitions to clients about their right to confront and to demand that their families listen. Although it wasn't my intention to alienate clients from their families, that is in fact what occurred as time and time again survivors confronted their families and demanded to be believed.

Now, 10 years later, I realize that there are better ways to confront family members and more conducive ways of helping family members out of their denial. Those of you who know me by my previous books related to childhood sexual abuse, *The Right to Innocence: Healing the Trauma of Childhood Sexual Abuse*, *Divorcing a Parent*, and *Partners in Recovery*, will discover that a much more mellow, more forgiving, and more well-rounded person is writing this book, probably the last of my series on childhood sexual abuse.

To Family Members

Many of you will be reading this book with a suspicious eye. You probably don't know whether to believe all that you have heard about childhood sexual abuse, and you may be suspicious of therapists, particularly those who specialize in this field. I felt it might allay your suspicions if you knew a little bit about me and what I stand for.

As a survivor of childhood sexual abuse myself, I have experienced firsthand the pain, guilt, shame, anger, and fear associated with it. I personally have experienced many of the symptoms and long-term effects of abuse that I will be discussing in this book. And I myself experienced the pain of realizing that my mother did not understand my emotions as they came pouring out; nor did she recognize that many of my problems were aftereffects of the sexual abuse I had suffered. Instead she minimized the abuse and told me I should go on with my life and forget about it—as she always tried to do when anything bad happened to her.

For these and many other reasons, I stopped seeing my mother for two years. The pain of being around her was just too great. I wasn't trying to punish her but to protect myself. In those two years I became much stronger, and eventually I was able to reconnect with her, although I did it only a little bit at a time. My mother died a year and a half after we had reconciled, and much of that time she was incoherent and out of reach emotionally. While I do not blame myself for needing that time away, I deeply regret that we lost two of our last few years together.

My mother and I reconciled because we both had been working very hard on ourselves and because in spite of our problems we loved each other very much. We reconciled because we were each able to put aside our hurt and anger in the interest of the relationship. And, most important, we came back together because we stopped being so headstrong and stubborn and were able to admit the mistakes we had made.

Although our time together was limited, in the end my mother and I were able to be more honest, more forgiving, and more loving than we had ever been in my entire life. This made her passing less painful to both of us.

And so I want you to know that, aside from my being a psychotherapist who has specialized in the field of childhood sexual abuse for 19 years, I have a personal interest in helping you, as a family, to work together to heal from the devastating wounds of childhood sexual abuse.

Throughout the years, I have received many, many letters from family members of survivors who have read my book, The Right to Innocence. Many of these letters chastised me for being so hard on family members and perpetrators and for accusing the nonoffending parent of knowing about the abuse and thus being a "silent partner" to the abuse. Many were letters stating that I didn't understand how difficult it is for family members of survivors. And some of the letters were requests for me to write a book for family members to help them to get through this most difficult time. Although I had planned all along to write a book expressly for family members, these letters helped me to have a far better understanding of just what family members of survivors go through and what kind of help they need. I hope this book provides you with the kind of help and understanding that you deserve.

If someone in your family—your child, your sibling, your grandchild, or even your parent—was sexually abused, or if you suspect they were sexually abused, this book should be of great help to you. Every single person who is related to a sexual-abuse victim is affected by the sexual abuse either directly or indirectly. Every person in the family needs help in order to cope with the situation and heal from the damage.

If a relative has recommended that you read this book, it is probably because that relative was sexually abused as a child and this is their way of telling you. You may find that you are experiencing both a desire to put this book away and a curiosity about just what it has to say. For your sake, the sake of the survivor, and the sake of your entire family, I urge you to continue reading. Besides helping you cope with this alarming information, this book may either help you maintain a good relationship with this family member or repair a relationship that has been strained or broken for quite some time. ❖

1

HOPE FOR
THE FAMILY

Survivors of childhood sexual abuse need their families very much.
They need their families to believe them when they tell their families
they were sexually abused. They need their families to validate their
memories and their experience. They need their families to stand up for
them against the perpetrator and to support them by insisting that the
perpetrator get help. Survivors need their families to work with them to
insure that their children and any other children both inside and outside
the family are not endangered by being around the perpetrator. And, if they
were sexually abused by someone in the family, they desperately need that
person to admit the abuse, to apologize for the damage they caused, and
to come forward and admit the abuse to other family members.

Research shows that those victims of sexual abuse who have the support of
family recover much faster than those who do not. Unfortunately, most victims
of childhood sexual abuse have to struggle all alone, without the understanding and support of family. Often they are criticized for exposing the
abuse and causing trouble in the family, for the amount of time and money
they spend on therapy, or for being in therapy at all.

No matter how well-meaning, family members inadvertently say and do
things that hurt those they love. Out of fear or ignorance, or in an attempt
to maintain the status quo, they often say and do the exact opposite of
what the survivor actually needs. For example, family members may encourage survivors to forget the abuse and go on with their lives. Unfortunately,
since this is what the survivor has been trying to do without success, this kind
of advice only makes the survivor feel like a failure. Survivors of childhood

sexual abuse cannot just forget about the trauma and go on as if nothing had ever happened, because the abuse affects them every day of their lives.

Family members can actually interfere with a survivor's progress by giving inappropriate advice. For example, most people don't understand the amount of anger a survivor feels or that this anger must be ventilated in a constructive way before recovery can occur. Because most people are threatened by such rage and are brought up to believe we should repress our anger, survivors are criticized for being so angry—thus reinforcing their own doubts about their feelings.

Often survivors are encouraged by their therapists and by members of their support groups to do things that seem very bizarre, such as carrying around a stuffed animal or talking out loud to an imaginary perpetrator or writing with their less-dominant hand or coloring with crayons. Unless family members can understand the process the survivor is going through and the reasons behind it, they can't help but be fearful and critical.

When a family does not work together to confront the issue of childhood sexual abuse, the entire family suffers. In the past, when victims have confronted their families with the truth, they have been called liars and been accused of trying to hurt the family or of being delusional or crazy. They have been ignored, threatened, and ostracized from the family.

On the other side, victims have demanded that their families believe them and that they confront and then reject the perpetrator. They have tended to be accusatory, unrelenting in their demands, and impatient with their families' reluctance to listen to them and to believe them. When their families have not believed them, victims have become enraged to the point of disowning the family.

Many families have been torn apart because of childhood sexual abuse. Because of their denial, fear of the truth, pride, need to be right, guilt, and anger, family members have turned away from one another at a time when they needed each other the most. Family members have said things to one another they never imagined they would say, have stopped speaking to one another, or even disowned one another over the issue of childhood sexual abuse.

The way it has been in the past is not the way it needs to be. Just as victims can become survivors, families can also survive childhood sexual abuse. Victims can learn to tell their families about their abuse in ways that encourage honesty and openness instead of distrust and denial. Families can learn to listen without being defensive, to take responsibility without guilt or blame, and to communicate with one another in ways that encourage healing. Victims can learn to be more patient with their families without compromising their own integrity. They can learn to demand the truth without alienating their families and express their emotions without being abusive themselves. Family members can learn to examine their motives for not believing the survivor—a process that includes exploring their own histories for signs of abuse.

To their credit, relatives of survivors often want to help but don't know how. *Families in Recovery* is intended to bring families back together, to help them heal from the devastation of childhood sexual abuse, and to help break the cycle of abuse that will undoubtedly continue unless there is intervention and cooperation between all family members.

There will of course still be parents who refuse to believe their adult children when they tell them they were sexually abused. There will be siblings who refuse to believe that their parent, grandparent, or another sibling could be a child molester. And there will be families who refuse to work together to overcome the damage childhood sexual abuse has done. But we have come so far in our understanding of childhood sexual abuse that I choose to believe these situations will someday be the exception to the rule.

CHILDHOOD SEXUAL ABUSE IS A FAMILY PROBLEM

Childhood sexual abuse touches every person in a family, not just the victim. If a loved one has been hurt, we hurt along with him, but there is more to it than that. Sexual abuse is a family problem, stemming from family dynamics, and is passed on to the next generation. Each member of the family suffers because of the emotions the abuse elicits or because of the influence it has on the relationships in the family or because of its long-term effects on each member.

In this book I directly address the specific concerns of each family member—the nonoffending parent, siblings or other relatives, and the perpetrator, as well as the survivor herself. Each member has specific issues concerning the abuse that need to be addressed in-depth. Survivors are offered suggestions as to the best ways to break the news of their abuse to family members. Family members are advised how to respond to a survivor when he or she tells them about the abuse so as to facilitate communication and encourage family unity. And both the survivor and those in her family are given suggestions as to how best to support one another throughout the recovery process.

When sexual abuse occurs within the family, it affects the entire family, whether or not each member is consciously aware that it is going on. There is added tension in the home as the abuser works hard to hide what he is doing and as the rest of the family unconsciously attempts to deny that anything is wrong. Whether family members know about the abuse or are only subconsciously aware of it, everyone feels the stress of hiding such a secret. Tension between family members is increased as each member struggles to cope with his pain, guilt, and anger.

When a child in a family is sexually abused, she or he feels many things, most of all shame and guilt. The child may feel like she is bad, that she is damaged goods or that she is a sinner. These feelings will frequently cause victims to distance themselves from those they love the most because they feel they are no longer worthy of being loved. Because they feel ugly, dirty, or rotten inside, they will often assume that their family could not possibly still love them.

A mother who is aware that her husband is paying an inordinate amount of attention to their daughter may feel jealous of the daughter. She may begin to see her daughter as competition rather than as a child who needs her protection. She may become hostile toward her daughter, thus indirectly encouraging her to seek love and attention from the father.

Abusive fathers or stepfathers often deliberately turn the family against the victim, thus ensuring easy access to the child and little or no support for her from the rest of the family. It is a common tactic on the part of the abusive father to encourage a split between his daughter and his wife. In this way he can guarantee that his daughter will not tell her mother and that even if she does tell, his wife will not believe her.

Although most mothers do nothing to stop their husband or lover from continuing to abuse their children, some mothers do stand up for their children when they learn of the abuse. If a divorce or separation occurs as a result of such discovery, however, the mother and the entire family may blame the child for the breakup of the family.

Siblings are often jealous of the attention given the victim by the perpetrator, not understanding the huge price she is paying for such attention or the reason why the perpetrator is giving it. Even those siblings who know about the sexual abuse may secretly feel that the victim got what she deserved or that she asked for it.

When sibling abuse occurs, the rest of the family often views the experience as an embarrassment, something to hide, rather than an attack on the younger child. The younger child, especially if it is a female, is often ostracized from the family and seen as a whore or a seductress. Both mother and father may distance themselves from her or become physically or emotionally abusive to her as a way of acting out their anger.

When parents, siblings, or other family members learn of the sexual abuse, their feelings toward the victim often change dramatically. Parents may feel ashamed of the situation and even of their child. They may treat the victim as if she is damaged goods or as if she was somehow to blame for the abuse. Siblings may be so embarrassed by the situation that they distance themselves from the victim. Or family members may just feel helpless and not know what to say or do.

Few family members recognize that any acting out on the part of the victim is usually a symptom of the abuse. If a victim acts out sexually, by appearing to be seductive or by becoming promiscuous, family members may take this as evidence that the victim asked for the abuse all along, instead of recognizing it as a side effect of the abuse itself. This was the case with Lee Ann:

"After I was sexually abused by my stepfather, I didn't care about anything anymore. I started going out with any boy who asked and having sex with all of them. Pretty soon, boys were practically lining up at my door to go out with me. My mother would just look at me and shake her head. She never said anything about what I was doing. She could have stopped me—after all, I was just 13. But she didn't. She was ashamed of me, and I know she just thought I was a whore. My sisters called me a tramp and were embarrassed to be seen with me at school. It makes me so angry now to realize that no one even tried to help me or to understand what was going on with me."

Children who have been sexually abused often take out their anger on those who are less powerful than themselves, such as their younger siblings, younger playmates, or their pets. This acting-out behavior can also alienate the family from the victim, since no one likes a bully or a troublemaker. Not understanding why the victim has changed, parents and siblings may begin to dislike this child and thus distance themselves from her or him.

And so we see a picture of a family entirely disrupted by the sexual abuse of one child. We see family bonds strained or even broken as members turn away from the victim in disgust and embarrassment, as daughters are torn away from their mothers, as normal sibling rivalry turns to hatred, and an entire family pays the price for harboring a criminal.

When a child is sexually abused, that child will suffer from devastating wounds to his or her body, mind, and soul. The short-term effects are only outweighed by the many long-term effects. It will literally take a lifetime for a victim of childhood sexual abuse to recover. The same is true of the victim's family. They, too, will suffer devastating wounds. And just as it takes time for a victim of childhood sexual abuse to recover, it will take time for the victim's family to recover. Last but certainly not least, just as the victim needs help in order to recover, the victim's family also needs help. *Families in Recovery* offers the entire family—parents, siblings, grandparents, aunts, uncles, cousins—the help they so desperately need in order to heal from the wounds of childhood sexual abuse.

For example, the nonoffending parent needs help to understand why she didn't know the abuse was going on, why she didn't "see" abuse even when it was occurring right in front of her, why she didn't act on her suspicions, why she stood by while the abuse occurred, or why she wasn't able to leave the situation when she discovered her child was being abused. She needs help so she won't be so defensive but can instead admit her mistakes, work with her guilt in a constructive way, and therefore be more free to help her adult child *now*.

Siblings also need to deal with their guilt—either because they didn't try to help, because they were glad it wasn't them, or because they always resented the survivor for being "the favorite one."

And perpetrators need help so they can admit they sexually abused a family member and that they need professional therapy.

How This Book Can Help

Families in Recovery is divided into three parts. Part I, "Coping with the News," deals with the family's initial reaction to hearing that someone in the family was sexually abused. It begins with a section specifically for the survivor, suggesting ways of breaking the news without alienating the family. General reactions are discussed, and then each member of the family is addressed individually.

Part II, "How to Support Each Other Throughout Recovery," will provide survivors with suggestions as to how they can best support members of their family, recognizing that they, too, will be recovering from the abuse. In addition, it will discuss the various ways that each member of the family can support the survivor and one another as they each go through the recovery process. The recovery process itself will be explained so that each family member will better understand what survivors must go through and what to expect as their relative goes through therapy or a 12-step recovery program. It will explain to them how they can best support the survivor throughout the healing process.

In Part III, "Bringing the Family Back Together," the issue of separated or divorced families will be discussed. This section is for those families who have had a difficult time believing that the abuse actually occurred (because they feel that to acknowledge it means choosing one family member over another) or who have been unable to sever their relationship with the perpetrator, even though they believe the abuse did occur.

The book will conclude with a chapter entitled "Working Together for a Healthier Family," in which the issues of learning better communication and changing negative patterns will be discussed. Included in this chapter will be information on how individual, conjoint, and family therapy can help your family heal from the damage of childhood sexual abuse and become a healthier family unit.

Starting with Part I, I will help families avoid some common early mistakes that hamper the recovery process. Families who have known for some time that a family member was sexually abused may want to skip to Part II. Those families who have been torn apart by the abuse and alienated from one another for some time may want to begin the book by reading Part III and working their way backward.

I have divided each part into two major sections, "For the Survivor" and "For Family Members," giving separate advice to each. I address the survivor first because the way he or she goes about the process of breaking the silence, supporting other family members, or attempting to reconcile after a separation or divorce will strongly affect the outcome of each task. I also address the survivor first because survivors are likely to be the ones buying the book in the first place and then passing it on to their families. The point here is that each member of the family, the survivor included, has a tremendous responsibility to work with other family members toward the healing of the family.

I suggest that each family member read both the advice to the survivor and the advice to other family members to get a better perspective on each other's struggle and as a reminder that family members must work together to overcome the devastation of childhood sexual abuse. (If you do read both sections, you may experience some redundancy.)

Although many victims of childhood sexual abuse are males, I will primarily refer to victims as "she." By the same token, while we know that the perpetrators of this crime are sometimes female, for easier reading I will refer to them as "he."

In addition, victims will be referred to primarily as "survivors," since most prefer to be viewed as having survived a traumatic event and thus having earned such a title. The word "perpetrator" is used to refer to the sexual abuser, denoting the fact that childhood sexual abuse is indeed a crime. Please refer to appendix I for other commonly used terms and their definitions, as well as pertinent background information.

Learning that a relative was sexually abused in childhood can have a profound effect, creating a crisis within the entire family. But it is possible to work through this crisis without blame, denial, or minimization and without creating a split in the family. It is possible to acknowledge that the abuse occurred without your family's falling completely apart. And it is possible to support the survivor even though she is full of anger—toward the perpetrator, the rest of the family, and even you. It is not only possible but essential that you learn to support the survivor's right to have all her emotions—anger, sadness, fear, guilt, shame, and grief—and that you allow yourself this privilege as well. It is possible for you to begin to view the accused molester through clear eyes, not blinded by denial, lies, or a need to maintain the status quo. It is possible to see the perpetrator as he really is—not as you would like him to be or as he would like you to see him—and to recognize that he is a complicated human being who has committed a serious transgression and who needs to be held accountable for it but who also needs to undergo treatment. And it is possible that with your help, your family can break the cycle of abuse and make certain that it doesn't get passed down to one more generation.

PART I

COPING WITH THE NEWS

When the silence is broken concerning childhood sexual abuse, emotions may erupt, family members may react in unpredictable ways, and the entire family system may be threatened.

The worst-case scenario might be that all members of a survivor's family deny that the abuse took place and believe that the survivor is "making it up," is "crazy," or has been "brainwashed" by her therapist. In a more hopeful scenario, family members meet the challenge that is presented to them, look at their own personal issues, and respond to the survivor with an honest attempt to believe, to understand, and to support. When this occurs, healing can happen and the family can survive, recover, and thrive.

2

How to Break the News to Your Family

For the Survivor

If you are a survivor of sexual abuse, you more than likely have read many other books on the subject of sexual abuse. Some of these books may have dealt with the issue of breaking the silence, telling your family about the abuse, and confronting your perpetrator and other family members with your anger and hurt. But the information you have read in these books, including my book *The Right to Innocence*, has all been aimed at helping you, the survivor, to break the silence and to finally rid yourself of the secrets that have been weighing you down, without much regard for how your family might respond to your telling. The material in this and other chapters specifically for the survivor will be distinctly different from other books in that it attempts to both support you and to help you to be cognizant of how the news will affect other family members. It is important to remember that at times these two things are mutually exclusive. Often, survivors need to just think of themselves, because when they begin to consider the feelings of family members they get lost and put their own needs aside. If this is your situation, then be forewarned that the following information may confuse you and therefore may not apply to you. If, however, you can maintain your sense of self while reaching out to your family, the following information will help you to that end.

If you feel you are ready to tell your family or some members of your family about the fact that you were sexually abused as a child there are a few questions you will need to ask yourself:

- What is my intention in telling one or more members of my family?
- How do I think they will react?
- What is my goal concerning the interaction?

Depending upon what your intention or motive is, you may or may not be setting yourself up for failure or disappointment. If your intention is to force a family member into admitting that they knew about the abuse all along, you will more than likely be disappointed, since this seldom happens. If your intention is to have one of your parents (or another caretaker) tell you that they recognize they did not protect you well enough to prevent the abuse, you will likewise be disappointed. And if you plan on getting an apology or admission of guilt from your perpetrator you are not being realistic at all. Few perpetrators will ever admit guilt, even when they are caught in the act.

But if, on the other hand, your intention is to get it off your chest, let go of the secret, share this meaningful event with a family member so that you no longer have to feel so alone, then there is little possibility for disappointment. You have accomplished your goal no matter what your family member's reaction is just by the mere fact that you have told him or her about your abuse. If your goal in telling the perpetrator that you remember the abuse is to stand up to him once and for all with the truth, then you have accomplished that goal in the telling, regardless of his or her reaction.

It is extremely important that you be as realistic as possible when you anticipate how a family member will react. Nine times out of ten, survivors do not receive the support and understanding they need and want, but instead are faced with questions and doubt, if not disbelief. If, for example, you fantasize your mother breaking down and crying for your pain, reaching out to hold you close to her, telling you that she believes you and that she will stand behind you all the way—you are indeed in fantasyland. While it is important to know what you would like to have happen, it is equally important to remind yourself that the chances are high that you will not receive what you need and hope for.

If, on the other hand, you imagine that your parent will have a difficult time with the idea and that she will need time to take it all in and to get over the shock, especially if the perpetrator is another relative of yours, then you are being realistic.

While it is good to be realistic, some survivors go to the other extreme and go into the situation expecting the worst. They want their parent(s), siblings, or other family members to know about their abuse, but they are afraid of their reaction. They are convinced they will not be believed or that they'll be told it was their fault or advised to forgive and forget. They are certain the family member will not understand how much they need their support and will minimize their pain and suffering.

"I was so afraid to tell my mother that my father had sexually abused me," recalls Susan. "I was afraid she wouldn't believe me, that she would call me a liar, that she would take my father's side. I thought for sure that it might be the end of my relationship with both my parents."

If this is your situation, it is important to know that by anticipating such a reaction you may in fact set up the situation so that your worst fears come true. Although you can certainly anticipate a family member's reaction based on their past reactions, you can't in all honesty know exactly how he or she is going to respond. There is always a possibility that the person may surprise you and react in a far more positive way than you ever anticipated. Staying open to this possibility will allow for a positive exchange.

Much to Susan's surprise, her mother didn't call her a liar but instead wanted to know more details about the abuse. After taking some time to think, Susan's mother called her on the phone and told her that she believed her, that what she had told her made sense and that it explained a lot of things to her.

DECIDING WHOM TO TELL FIRST

Some survivors have chosen to break the silence with the family member they feel closest to, or the one they expect will support them the most. If a particular family member is especially open to you and is likely to believe you, a supportive bond can be established immediately. By contacting this family member early on in your recovery process you may receive much-needed validation and support throughout your recovery. When the going gets rough, an ally within the family may be the most valuable asset a survivor has.

For example, some survivors choose to tell their siblings first in order to elicit support before they tackle telling a nonoffending parent, especially if they have reason to believe that another sibling was also abused by the same perpetrator.

On the other hand, it may be a risk to tell your closest relative, because if this family member's initial response is negative and the relationship is strained or even severed, you will be left feeling extremely alone without an ally in the family.

Some survivors want to get it over with and so choose to tell the family member they expect will be hardest to tell. Telling a nonoffending parent that her spouse sexually abused you has got to be one of the hardest things to do, but some survivors feel that after they have accomplished this the worst is over. Because telling their siblings and other family members will not be as difficult, they feel they can do so in their own time, whenever they feel it is appropriate.

SETTING THE STAGE

Many survivors bombard their families with the information that they were sexually abused, with little or no warning. This causes family members to react more intensely and more defensively than they would normally. If you would like to do the telling without disrupting your family unnecessarily, it will be important to do it right.

Call or write ahead of time the family member you wish to talk to. Tell him or her that you have something very important to talk about and set up a time for a meeting. Ideally, set it up so that you and the other family member will be able to talk privately without interference from anyone else. Make certain that you put aside enough time for processing the feelings that will undoubtedly emerge after you have revealed your abuse.

If you are in therapy and you would feel more comfortable, break the silence in your therapist's office. But be aware that while having your therapist there supporting you will make you feel more comfortable, it may make your relative feel exposed and extremely uncomfortable.

When you meet, tell the family member that what you have to tell her will shock and upset her, but that it is very important that she knows this information. If you feel loving toward her, tell her so before you plunge in. Knowing that you love her may help her to digest the information more easily. Also, these words may soften the blow, especially if there are angry words exchanged after you tell.

After you tell, recognize that your relative will need time to absorb the information and process her feelings. Just because a family member doesn't respond the way you would like them to in the moment doesn't mean they aren't capable of doing so at a later time. Remember that while you have spent a lot of time with your feelings about the abuse, this information may be completely new to them. Even if they really did know all along, the fact that *you* have come forward is news to them.

Don't try to resolve all your issues in one sitting. It is unrealistic of you to expect your relative to do any of the following in this first meeting: state that they believe you, choose you over the perpetrator, ask your forgiveness for not protecting you, admit that they abused you. Your relative is going to have to revise their perceptions of the perpetrator, of you, of themselves, and of the entire family, and this will take time. If you handle this first meeting properly, this will be the first of many conversations about the abuse. Your relative will probably be completely overwhelmed with the information and may need time alone now. You, too, will need time alone to absorb the fact that you have finally told.

How to Tell So That You Are Really Heard

If your intention in telling a family member about the abuse is not to punish or point fingers, then the way you tell them will reflect this. If, on the other hand, you tell in an accusatory, blaming, or angry way, you will create a defensive environment where the person you are telling has no choice but to become defensive.

Although you may undoubtedly be angry at different family members for not protecting you, for not believing you when you tried to tell before, or for continuing a relationship with the perpetrator, this is not the time to tell them about your anger. Your focus now must be solely on breaking the silence.

There certainly is a time and place for you to tell them about your anger toward them, but the focus of this chapter is about breaking the news in such a way that your family members can really hear you. It doesn't matter whether they *should* have known or whether you think they *did* know all along, what matters now is that you tell them about your experience of abuse. Although other family members will undoubtedly need to be told, I have focused on telling mothers and siblings because they are the ones most often told and told first. Generally speaking, they are also the ones who can hurt you the most if they turn against you.

Telling Your Mother

While it makes sense that you would feel angry at your mother for not protecting you better, if your mother feels like you are blaming her she will naturally become defensive. She will especially become guarded if she feels you are blaming her for something she has not actually done.

After you tell your mother about the abuse, sit back and watch and listen to her response before you jump in with accusations. Although you may be completely convinced that she did in fact know about the abuse all along, listen to what she has to say about it and then evaluate the situation again.

Most victims of childhood sexual abuse feel betrayed by their mother and feel she should have protected them better. This is natural since we hold mothers primarily responsible for the protection and care of their children. Although in fact your mother may not have protected you sufficiently, and you can argue that she should have known the abuse was occurring, she didn't necessarily know about it.

If the abuse was done in front of her or if she walked in while it was occurring, if she participated in the abuse, or if you showed obvious signs and symptoms of abuse that she ignored (bleeding; red, swollen genitals; bruises; constant crying), then you certainly have every indication that she did in fact know. Otherwise you do not know for a fact that she knew and it is not only unfair of you to assume this but this presumption will get in the way of you and your mother being able to work together toward recovery.

Try to distinguish the anger you feel toward your mother from the anger you feel toward the perpetrator. Your mother doesn't deserve the blame for what the perpetrator did. Unless she is in fact the abuser, she is responsible only for her part in the abuse, not the actual abuse itself.

TELLING YOUR SIBLINGS

The important thing in telling your siblings about the abuse is to remember that they, like you, were members of a dysfunctional family and they, like you, were victims of emotional, physical, and/or sexual abuse; children of alcoholics, or children of emotionally disturbed parents. The second thing to remember is that your sibling was not responsible for you.

It doesn't matter whether your sibling was older than you, was put in charge of you, or even if you viewed a much older sibling as a surrogate parent; that sibling was in fact not a parent.

Carmen was extremely angry with her older sister Maria. She blamed her for not stopping her father from sexually abusing her. Since their mother had died when Carmen was small and her sister Maria was seven years older than her, Carmen viewed her more as a mother than as a sister. When she told Maria at nine years old that her father was raping her, she fully expected her to put a stop to it. But Maria only told her to try to stay away from her father as much as possible. Carmen felt so betrayed by her sister that she never forgave her. Now, as an adult, Carmen still holds her sister responsible for the fact that her father continued to abuse her for four more years.

It wasn't until Carmen brought Maria into therapy with her that she began to fully understand the situation. Maria had been sexually abused by their father also and was terribly afraid of him. She felt badly for her sister when she learned that he was abusing her also, but she couldn't do anything about it.

It took a long time for Carmen to understand that even though Maria seemed like a mother to her, she was in fact, just a child herself, as dependent as she was on her father to take care of her.

With patience and foresight, you can make breaking the silence a positive experience for you and even for other family members. Just remember the following as you develop your plan of action:

- Focus on breaking the silence, not on blaming anyone in the family at this point
- Don't assume that a family member knew
- Don't hold anyone responsible for what the perpetrator did but the perpetrator himself.

3

COPING WITH THE NEWS

For Family Members

Whether you are the mother, the father, the sibling, the grandparent, the aunt or uncle, the cousin, the niece or nephew, or the child of the survivor, your image of the "perfect" or "normal" family will be shaken and your life will be thrown into turmoil by the news that someone in your family was sexually abused. You will undoubtedly have many strong feelings and reactions to this devastating news. You may not believe it at first. After all, it is quite shocking to realize that something as traumatic as this happened to someone you cared about and you didn't even know about it. You may feel enraged—with the perpetrator, with those who should have been protecting the child, or even at the survivor. You may feel tremendously guilty or responsible, or you may feel blamed. You may feel devastated—for the survivor, for other family members, or for yourself. You may feel a deep sorrow and compassion for the pain the survivor must suffer. This in turn may remind you of the sorrow and pain you have felt sometime in your life at having been victimized. You may feel helpless, confused, hopeless, or just numb. You may feel betrayed by the perpetrator or even by the survivor.

In addition to all these feelings, you will be faced with agonizing choices—whom to believe, whom to continue a relationship with, whom to maintain a loyalty to. If the survivor is accusing another family member of abusing her, you will probably feel you must choose to stand by one person while forsaking another, to believe one person's word while essentially calling the other a liar. It is seldom possible or even advisable to maintain a middle ground in this situation.

In addition, you will be forced to revise your perceptions of the victim, the abuser, the relationships within your family, and even your perceptions of yourself. This can of course be terribly disruptive, disorienting, and anxiety-provoking. We tend to feel threatened and vulnerable when our beliefs about ourselves are challenged.

QUESTIONS AND ANSWERS

The following are the most common questions family members have when they learn that someone in the family was sexually abused. By answering each question, I hope to help you overcome some of your resistance to this news and get on with the difficult process of healing.

WHY DIDN'T MY CHILD (OR SIBLING) TELL SOONER?

This is indeed a valid question. One can't help but wonder why a child wouldn't tell her parent when she is hurt in such a horrible way, why a child wouldn't automatically turn to her family for comfort. It is even more baffling to consider why the child would continue to keep this secret from her family as an adult. But while it is natural to wonder at these things, it will make the survivor feel you don't believe her if you ask her these questions.

There are many reasons why sexually abused children don't tell while they are children:

- They have been threatened by their abuser, who they feared might kill them, their parents, or their pets.
- They are afraid that no one will believe them. They may have

already had the experience of telling their parents the truth only to be accused of making it up. They believe that their word alone would very likely not be honored.

- They are afraid they will be blamed.
- They are afraid they will be punished. (Children who are sexually abused often have a history of being severely punished for even the slightest mistake.)
- They feel there is no use in telling. If their parents are rarely around or are preoccupied with their own lives, children may feel that their parents simply don't care what happens to them.
- They feel such guilt and shame that they just can't tell. This is especially true if their body responded to the sexual stimulation. They fear that anyone they might tell would surely blame them as much as they blame themselves.
- They feel that somehow their mother must already know about what is going on, and therefore they feel too betrayed to tell.
- They are afraid their mother will divorce their father (the abuser) if they tell. Many victims fear being sent to a foster home.
- They wish to protect the perpetrator.

WHY DIDN'T SHE TELL WHEN SHE BECAME AN ADULT?

The most common reason why survivors of sexual abuse do not tell when they are adults is because they do not remember the abuse. This can be true for two reasons. First of all, when a child is being traumatized, the emotional, physical, and psychic trauma is so severe that they dissociate, or leave their bodies, in order to protect themselves. The child dissociates by thinking of something else—by distracting herself—sometimes withdrawing into herself so completely that she blocks out all feeling. Although the child's body is still present, her mind is elsewhere, and thus she may not even have a memory of what occurred. Her body was still present while the abuse occurred and so her body has a memory of what happened but not her mind. Instead, the memory is filed away somewhere out of reach.

In addition, repression is a common defense against having to face the pain of severely traumatic events. Just as accident victims often experience a temporary or sometimes even permanent amnesia regarding the details of the accident, children who are sexually abused often block out or forget the incident(s).

WHY ARE THE MEMORIES SURFACING NOW?

Long-repressed, traumatic memories usually do not surface until the person is emotionally strong enough to handle them. The unconscious yields formerly inaccessible information when the survivor can finally cope with its magnitude. Perhaps the survivor has achieved enough personal growth through therapy or a 12-step program or has an environment that is safe and supportive enough to give her the strength to finally face the truth.

Sometimes, the survivor's defense system simply wears down. For whatever reason, she no longer has the energy to continue holding back the secrets and the lies. Perhaps she has become overloaded with other problems (work, marriage, money) or is no longer able to find relief in the coping strategies that helped in childhood. Perhaps she is newly sober and is being bombarded with memories that she previously drowned with alcohol or drugs.

Often survivors' memories are triggered by something in their environment. It is common for survivors to regain their memories when their own child reaches the age when they themselves were molested. Other environmental cues include a friend's recounting experiences of sexual abuse, a television talk show on the subject, a visit with a family member, a visit to an old neighborhood, or a family reunion.

HOW DO MEMORIES SURFACE?

Memories surface in many different ways. The most common way is through flashbacks—a reliving of an event through one or more of the senses. During a flashback, one seems to see, feel, smell, or taste something from the past as if it were actually happening in the present. The survivor may visualize certain elements of the abuse or feel sensations related to it (vaginal, pelvic, or anal pain, tingling, gagging, smothering, or the sensation of someone's hands on them) as if it were happening now. They may hear someone breathe, cry, or snore as if they were present in the room they are occupying. Some survivors have olfactory flashbacks, wherein they smell things associated with the abuse, such as after-shave or perspiraton. Some experience emotional flashbacks—a reexperiencing of overwhelming fear, pain, or confusion, often out of proportion to the event occurring in the present.

Flashbacks are a clearing process of the mind. Like certain dreams, they provide a way for the unconscious to bypass both memory blocks and the defense mechanism of dissociation. In the recovery process, a flashback can be an important part of remembering. Flashbacks may occur at any time without notice or in conjunction with some related circumstances—during intercourse or sexual foreplay, for instance, or even during childbirth, dental work, surgery, or massage. (All of these situations require us to surrender control and to trust someone else to perform a procedure. Dental work frequently triggers memories for those who were orally raped.)

Though the mind may repress or deny the reality of the abuse, the body always stores the memory and gives the greatest testimony to its occurrence. *The body never forgets.*

My relative says she (he) was abused by a female. Does this really happen, and if so, how?

Although most sexual offenses against children are perpetrated by males, many children are molested by females. In fact, as more and more reports of child sexual abuse are made, we are discovering that there are more female perpetrators than we ever imagined. Children have been sexually abused by their mothers, grandmothers, aunts, older sisters, older cousins, baby-sitters, older girls in the neighborhood, and female teachers and coaches.

The most common type of childhood sexual abuse perpetrated by females is that of mothers molesting their small children. These mothers, especially the ones who molest their infants and toddlers, are often emotionally disturbed or even psychotic or they may be reenacting the sexual abuse that they experienced as a child. Mothers have been known to fondle or suck their children's genitals, insert objects into their vaginas or anuses, or force the child to fondle or suck their breasts or genitals. Many of these mothers project their shame onto their daughters, seeing them as bad and dirty. Viewing their daughter's genitals as dirty, they may scrub them until they are raw. These same mothers often give frequent, unnecessary enemas to both their male and female children and perform frequent "inspections" of their children's genitals, under the auspices of looking for pinworms or other parasites.

Some mothers, emotionally isolated as children and incapable of expressing affection appropriately, see their children, especially their daughters, as extensions of themselves. They may stimulate their daughters sexually in order to satisfy their own needs for pleasure or actually believe that their actions are demonstrations of affection.

With their male children they may reenact the abuse in the same ways that males do, this time being the one who has the power. Molesting their son may be the only time they feel powerful over a male. Mother-son incest is probably the most subtly traumatic of all forms of incest. Since the incestuous mother cannot easily force her son, she must use seductiveness. This seductiveness turns out to be deadly, since the boy can't help but respond and then feels horribly guilty afterward. The long-term effects of this kind of abuse range from impotency to self-destructiveness or the victim, who may be resentful of women, may become a child molester, a rapist, or even a murderer.

Another type of sexual abuse performed by mothers and other female caretakers is what I call participatory abuse. This is when the mother participates in an act of child sexual abuse with a father, a sibling, or another male perpetrator. Often the male is the instigator and cajoles or forces the woman to take part.

Other female caretakers who molest children—both boys and girls—include baby-sitters. Often these baby-sitters are young girls who are themselves victims of childhood sexual abuse and are taking advantage of the fact that they have power over someone weaker than themselves. A number of adult males who were sexually abused by female baby-sitters don't identify the act as abuse. When I ask them whether they were ever sexually abused, many of my male clients will say no, but when I ask them to describe their first sexual experience, they will reveal that they were introduced to sex by a female baby-sitter when they were as young as two, three, or four years old. Because they sometimes remember feeling physically aroused by the experience, they consider it a good thing that happened to them, as if they got a head start on sex. These males don't understand the damage caused by becoming sexualized at such an early age, and the betrayal of trust involved.

Female baby-sitters or older neighborhood girls may also introduce girls younger than themselves to sex. These experiences may be all the more traumatic since they may cause the girl to doubt her sexuality. In general, girls are taught to feel more guilt-ridden about sex than boys, and a girl in this situation will tend to blame herself for allowing it to happen.

While sexual abuse by older sisters is less common than abuse by older brothers, it does occur. Even though an older female would have difficulty forcing a younger male to have intercourse with her, she may be so seductive that the younger male cannot control his urges. Some older sisters have used force, holding down their captives while they fondle them, perform oral sex on them, or insert objects into their anus.

MY RELATIVE TELLS ME SHE WAS ABUSED BY ANOTHER CHILD. HOW IS THAT POSSIBLE?

Not all sexual abuse is perpetrated by adults. More and more cases of sexual abuse perpetrated by other children are being reported every day. Children are sexually abused by older friends, neighbors, schoolmates, siblings, and cousins.

Sexual contact between one child and another who is younger or weaker is often misunderstood as "sex play." But normal sex play and exploration can occur only between those of the same age, sexual experience, and power. For example, when two consenting children of the same age "play doctor," this is likely to represent normal sexual experimentation, while sexual activity between a child of eight and an adolescent of fourteen is considered sexual abuse.

The majority of child perpetrators were themselves sexually abused and are reenacting their abuse with other children, either as a way of acting out their feelings or as a way of feeling empowered. Having been traumatized themselves and overpowered by someone stronger than themselves, they are acting out their anger and pain by abusing someone less powerful than themselves.

IS THERE SUCH A THING AS SIBLING ABUSE? AREN'T BOTH CHILDREN EQUALLY RESPONSIBLE IN CASES OF INCEST?

In most cases, incest between siblings is in fact sexual abuse, since it most often occurs when an older sibling coerces, threatens, or forces a younger sibling into sexual acts that the younger child is ill-equipped to handle. Even a sibling who is only two or three years older is both physically and emotionally stronger than the younger one, and thus there is an inequity of power. This gives the older sibling just enough of an edge to be able to overpower the younger sibling both physically and emotionally.

In some cases, even a one-year age difference between siblings can have enormous power implications for both parties. For example, an older brother is almost always seen as the authority figure, even when he is only a few years older. He is often left in charge of his younger sister, and in most families, females are taught to concede to the males. In addition, males are physically stronger, and their superior strength can be physically intimidating to a younger sister, especially if the brother tends to be a bully. The sister goes along with what he wants out of fear or a need to gain his approval.

There are also cases where the older sister is the aggressor, although this does not happen quite as often. But if a sister is quite a bit older, or if she is given more power in the family than the brother, either because she is seen as the younger sibling's caretaker or because females are honored more in the family, she can coerce or force her younger sibling into sexual activity just as a male sibling can.

Sexual abuse also occurs between same-sex siblings. Older brothers have been known to abuse their younger brothers, and older sisters to molest their younger sisters, but this doesn't occur as frequently as other types of sibling abuse. Again, such incidents should not be confused with sex play or exploration among same-age peers.

In many cases, older siblings are reenacting the sexual abuse that they have experienced. Many a child molester begins his lifelong career by making his younger sibling his first victim. Only under certain specific circumstances is sibling incest *not* sexual abuse:

- The children are young and approximately the same age
- They have equal power, both with each other and in the family
- There is no coercion or physical force
- The sexual play is the result of natural curiosity, exploration, and mutual sexual naïveté
- The children are not traumatized by disapproving parents who may "catch them in the act."

MY RELATIVE IS A MALE. CAN MALES REALLY BE SEXUALLY ABUSED?

It is a common misconception that far more girls are sexually abused than boys, and even when a boy is molested it doesn't affect him that much. But the latest figures indicate that one in three female children and one in four males have been sexually abused. Thus male children are sexually abused almost as often as female children. Because males tend to be even more reluctant to report experiences of child sexual abuse than females, the numbers may be even higher.

The sexual abuse of male children includes everything from an adult or older child exposing himself or herself to the child to forcible rape. It includes kissing the boy in a lingering or intimate way, masturbating in front of the child, fondling of the boy's genitals, thighs, or buttocks, forcing or coercing the boy to touch the perpetrator's genitals, performing oral sex on the boy or inducing the boy to perform oral sex on the perpetrator, and forcing his penis or other objects into the boys anus or forcing the boy to insert his penis or another object into the perpetrator's vagina or anus. It also includes parading around the house naked in front of the child, secretly observing the child while he bathes, undresses, or uses the toilet, or performing sexual acts in front of the boy.

DO MALE VICTIMS SUFFER IN THE SAME WAY AS FEMALE VICTIMS?

Although males and females suffer from the same long-term effects of childhood sexual abuse, males tend to react somewhat differently from females to the abuse itself. This is because we raise boys and girls differently, have different expectations of them, and tend to view male and female victims of sexual abuse differently.

Males in our culture are supposed to be dominant, aggressive, and confident, while females are traditionally viewed as submissive and passive. Males are supposed to be the seducers and controllers, while females are supposed to be the ones who are seduced or coerced into having sex. These distinctions add to the difficulties facing male survivors of sexual abuse.

Since women already are seen as passive beings, society more easily sympathizes with them when they are victimized. We have far more difficulty empathizing with male victims. Males are supposed to protect themselves (and others) in any situation, and if they are unable to do so, society views them as weak—the male victim is perceived as something less than a man, regardless of the situation.

Unfortunately, because of the expectations we so unfairly place on men, when a boy is sexually abused, he is in essence revictimized by his culture and his own tendency to be critical of himself. He sees himself as a coward for "allowing it to happen" in the first place and for not avenging the crime (something he obviously cannot do, because he is too afraid of his attacker, may not know how to find him, and if he does, would only be overpowered by him again). He sees himself as weak for not just forgetting it and putting it in the past (although he certainly tries).

Whether the perpetrator of the abuse was a male or a female, most male victims assume they must have done something to encourage the advances. Because most abusers are male, many male victims come to question their sexual orientation when they reach adolescence, even if the abuse occurred years earlier. They assume they must be homosexual for a man to have approached them to begin with.

Boys who were already aware of being attracted to other males, on the other hand, often reach manhood convinced that the sexual attack was just punishment for such homoerotic thoughts. Raised in a society that teaches them it is shameful to be gay, they have the added burden of shame arising from sexual victimization. Jason is a thirty-five-year-old gay man who is just beginning to accept his sexuality.

"I always blamed myself for being sexually abused because I had an adolescent crush on the man who molested me. He was my high-school wrestling coach, and I had fantasies about him all the time. When he started paying special attention to me, I was flattered. One day he asked me to help him out after school with some gym equipment, and he raped me—violently—in the equipment room. Years afterward, I felt

31

like I must have deserved rape for being attracted to a man. This incident made me hate myself for any homosexual feelings I had from that time on."

Some male survivors feel unable to define themselves as sexual beings at all, because sexuality has become associated with abuse in their minds. Terence's case is a good example: "My stepmother began to seduce me from the time she moved into our house when I was thirteen. She would walk around the house with hardly anything on, 'accidentally' walk in on me when I was in the bathroom, and was always having me rub her back, supposedly because it was sore. This behavior went on all during high school, when I should have been dating girls. I felt both turned on and repulsed by her, and this is how I still feel about women in general, fifteen years later. I can become attracted to them, but if they become the slightest bit aggressive with me, I lose all interest. I feel so ashamed about the feelings I had for my stepmother that I just can't seem to develop any confidence with a woman."

In our society, sexual activity between older women and younger boys is rarely treated as abusive. In fact, it is often glorified, as in the Louis Malle film *Murmur of the Heart*, where mother/son incest was portrayed as a laudable, tender affair. A boy who comes forward and talks about having been sexually abused by a woman is often greeted by police, doctors, the media, therapists, and even his family with disbelief or denial. They may trivialize or even romanticize his story. Faced with this situation, the boy may redefine his experiences to fit in with other people's perceptions, even to the point of bragging or joking about it.

All sexual-abuse victims suffer from low self-esteem and feelings of inferiority after having been abused. Many male victims tend to feel less masculine than other males or, worse, less human. Feeling branded and irreparably damaged, they believe no female would now want them. To counteract these feelings, many victims go to great lengths to prove their masculinity. They become sexually promiscuous, sexually violent, or overly controlling of women, or they attack other men they view as weaker than themselves. Some become daredevils, risking their lives to prove their manhood.

Because males are so embarrassed at having been sexually victimized, they cannot tolerate the feelings of helplessness that all victims feel. They short-circuit these feelings instead of identifying with other victims, and they identify with those who seem powerful—the abusers. This is the beginning of the vicious circle of sexually abused boys becoming sexually abusing men. (Women are more likely to repeat the cycle of abuse by continuing to be victimized.)

If the perpetrator of the sexual attack was a male and a primary role model, a male victim may well conclude that "being a man" means being abusive: he may believe he needs to inflict pain before it is inflicted on him. He further may conclude that the only way to empower himself is to make someone else a victim. As a result, many males who were sexually abused as children become child molesters themselves. This of course adds to the shame they already feel and further discourages them from seeking professional help.

Adult males suffer from a variety of sexual problems as a direct result of childhood sexual abuse. The most common are an inability to achieve or maintain an erection, premature ejaculation or an inability to ejaculate, fears of specific sexual acts (often those performed by the abuser or acts that the victims were forced to perform on the abuser), and painful intercourse. In addition, many male survivors suffer from sexual obsessions and fetishes, addiction to sex, compulsive masturbation, and a tendency to associate sex with humiliation and pain, which is the case with individuals who practice sadomasochism.

Armed with the above information, you should be a little more prepared to tackle the task at hand—that of working together with the survivor to heal his or her wounds and the wounds of the family.

BELIEVING WHAT YOU ARE HEARING

If this news is a total revelation to you, then it will indeed be a shock, particularly if you've never even imagined that such a thing could happen to your loved one. If the perpetrator is not a family member, you will probably have an easier time believing what your loved one is telling you. But if the perpetrator is a relative or someone else you are close to, the likelihood is strong that you will deny the whole issue. You may find yourself defending the perpetrator's character even though you never trusted him before. This kind of reaction is not so different from the way children often get angry at parents when they divorce, blaming the very parent who has endured abuse from her partner.

Although it is natural to experience disbelief and denial under these circumstances, please don't unequivocally dismiss the survivor's experience of sexual abuse as fantasy, lies, or delusions. Recognize that your immediate reaction may be based on your emotional need to keep your family from being disrupted. Although it is normal to want to keep your family intact and to try not to upset the status quo, you may be doing so at the price of the survivor's well-being and recovery.

By becoming aware of your protective reactions you will be less likely to view them as the truth. You will recognize that you need time to assimilate the information and to discover what this revelation means to you. Instead of undertaking a campaign to protect the perpetrator or to denounce the survivor's disclosure as lies, fantasies, or delusions, you can focus on honoring your own feelings. Take this time to talk with others outside the family about your reactions, confusion, and fears.

HOW DO I KNOW HE/SHE IS TELLING THE TRUTH?

While there have been isolated instances of children making false allegations, they are rare and usually involve child custody. Seldom if ever does an *adult* falsely claim to have been victimized as a child. After all, what purpose would it serve? The whole subject of child sexual abuse is so embarrassing that it's hard to imagine why anyone would fabricate such a story.

There have been accusations recently that therapists are "brainwashing" clients—convincing their clients that they were sexually abused, when in fact they were not. While there may have been some actual incidences of some overzealous therapists leading their clients or pushing then into remembering abuse experiences before they are ready to remember, the fact is that most therapists in the sexual abuse recovery field do not use methods such as hypnosis or repressed memory therapy. Most therapists, like myself, strive to provide a safe-enough environment where clients can uncover their memories in their own time, when they are strong enough to cope with them.

Most clients who have started therapy with me have come because they *suspect* they were sexually abused or already have their memories intact and want help recovering from the damage caused by such abuse.

Even when a client exhibits many of the symptoms that therapists have come to associate with sexual abuse, I, like most competent therapists, will wait for the client to come to this revelation on their own. Aside from pointing out the symptoms and asking if they were abused, most therapists do not try to convince their clients they were abused.

One good way of determining whether your relative is telling you the truth is to know how a victim of childhood sexual abuse typically behaves. In the following list of the long-term effects of childhood sexual abuse, the italicized items are the most common, and therefore the strongest warning signs. If your relative exhibits a majority of these italicized symptoms, you can be relatively certain she was in fact sexually abused.

1. **Difficulty trusting others.**
2. Intense anger and rage that sometimes burst out unexpectedly.
3. Mood swings ranging from deep depression to intense anxiety.
4. Low self-esteem, self-hatred, feeling ugly inside.
5. Guilt feelings and feelings of shame.

6. *"Somatic" symptoms:* Frequent sore throats; migraine headaches; "female problems," such as severe menstrual cramps, frequent vaginal infection, unexplained vaginal pain; frequent nausea; abdominal pain; skin disorders; disabling aches and pains or other symptoms often associated with tension, and unexplained pain or numbness in legs or arms.

7. *Sexual problems:* Lack of desire or sexual feelings and inability to enjoy sex or to have an orgasm. Problems with sexual identity, promiscuity, or continuing to be a sexual object. Attraction to "illicit" sexual activities.

8. Anger and disgust at any public display of affection, nudity, or partial nudity and any display of sexuality or nudity on television or in movies.

9. *Self-destructive behavior:* Attempted suicide, reckless driving, self-mutilation (scratching or picking at skin, cutting self with razor), self-starvation, binging and purging, compulsive eating, alcohol or drug abuse, compulsive gambling, involvement in destructive relationships.

10. Repeated involvement with people who inflict physical, verbal, emotional, or sexual abuse.

11. Chronic depression, causing excessive sleep, apathy, lethargy, hopelessness and suicidal thoughts.

12. **Dissociation** (a splitting off from self): **Time blockages** (sometimes long periods of time, even years, are "forgotten" and blocked from memory) and **feelings of numbness** in various parts of the body or even the entire body are also signs of dissociation.

13. *Extreme fears or phobias:* Claustrophobia (fear of closed places), an inordinate fear of going to the doctor or dentist, fear of taking a bath or shower, of going to sleep, of going to sleep with the door open (or closed), of sleeping with anyone, using public restrooms, or anything that triggers memories of childhood sexual abuse.

14. *Frequent nightmares, insomnia,* waking up at the same time every night and other sleep disturbances.

15. Fear, dizziness, or nausea triggered by certain smells, sights, sounds, or touches.
16. An inability to complete tasks, a tendency to sabotage success.
17. Lack of empathy or concern for others, feeling cut off from other people, a deep sense of isolation.
18. **Difficulty with physical affection:** Aversion to being touched or hugged, inability to express physical affection to loved ones. Fear of others' motives or of being misunderstood when affectionate.
19. **Tendency to be victimized by others, little or no sense of personal power, feelings of helplessness.**
20. Secrecy, evasiveness, and tendency to withhold information from others.
21. Tendency to "tell all." Because survivers of abuse had to "hold in" their terrible secret, they may now need to go to the opposite extreme of letting it all out—telling everyone their story even when it is not appropriate, being unable to keep a secret, or telling others how they feel about them, often to an extreme.
22. A tendency to "give yourself away": Helping others to the point of exhaustion and self-deprivation, giving away personal possessions, and becoming sexually involved with anyone who shows interest.
23. **Sexual manipulation:** Using sex, seductiveness, flirtation, or other sexual-manipulation techniques to get what one wants in marital, social, or business relationships; believing that in order to have a relationship one has to be sexual, sexualizing all relationships. This belief can cause survivors of abuse to victimize their own or other people's children.
24. **Addictions** to food, alcohol, drugs, or masturbation and other sexual activities.
25. **Obsessive/compulsive behavior:** Obsessive thoughts, compulsive cleaning, shopping, shoplifting, gambling, eating.
26. **Eating disorders: Anorexia** (slow suicide, need to disappear or be invisible), **obesity** (fear of being attractive, need to nurture self,

need for extra padding so one won't get hurt so much), *bulimia* (need to be in control of what goes into and out of one's body).

27. **Flashbacks, hallucinations** (suddenly being flooded with memories in the form of visual images, body sensations, dreams, sounds, smells): Flashbacks may be **visual** (seeing the scene), **tactile** (vaginal or pelvic pain, tingling, gagging, or smothering feelings), **auditory** (hearing somebody breathe, cry, snore) or **olfactory** (smelling body odors), may become more and more intense over time.

28. Difficulty with authority figures.

29. Difficulty communicating desires, thoughts, and feelings to others: Being at a loss for words, stuttering, stammering, and being afraid to speak in front of groups.

30. Difficulty receiving from others: Difficulty accepting presents, favors, or compliments.

31. Expecting others to show their love with presents or money (not believing they care unless they do).

32. **Abusive behavior:** Physically, verbally, emotionally, or sexually abusing others (including one's own children or animals).

33. Feelings of hopelessness, suicidal thoughts, or suicide attempts.

Exploring Your Own Family History

As I mentioned earlier, experts have come to realize that child sexual abuse is intergenerational, passed down from generation to generation within a family. This means that if one person in your family was sexually abused the likelihood is very strong that someone else in the family was also. And the person who is being accused has more than likely sexually abused other members of the family as well as others outside of the family. The perpetrator was more than likely sexually abused himself, perhaps by a family member.

If you are having a difficult time believing that something like this could happen in *your* family, spend some time exploring your family history. Was there anyone else in the family who was sexually abused? Was there a relative who was considered to be a "dirty old man," or a sex-maniac? Do you remember hearing whispers about a "strange" uncle or cousin? Did anyone in your family ever suffer from a mental disorder? Was anyone ever arrested or put in a mental hospital?

How can I believe without proof?

Requiring facts, times, and dates from your relatives suggests that you may remain skeptical even if you were provided with all of this information. Families have been known to deny and reject the truth even when more than one family member comes forward with reports of the abuse. If you are still doubtful at this point, be patient with yourself. You may be denying the reality of the survivor's abuse for some very good reason of your own. (Such reasons will be addressed in the next chapter.) Do not impose your skepticism on the survivor by dismissing the abuse because you can't deal with it yet.

The more you are exposed to the subject of child sexual abuse, either by reading about it or by listening to survivors, the less you will be inclined to disbelieve the survivor. The more stories you hear, the more facts you receive, the more you will realize that even though the things your loved one is telling you are hard for you to believe, such things do indeed occur.

If you are willing to spend time with the survivor and support her through her recovery process, you will find it difficult to deny the reality of her experience. No one can fake this process or the feeling. You will witness the survivor's gradual, painful growth and healing as she struggles through the process and achieves greater health and well-being.

I CAN'T BELIEVE THAT THE ACCUSED PERPETRATOR IS CAPABLE OF SEXUALLY ABUSING A CHILD.

It is difficult to determine just who is capable of molesting a child and who is not. Some of the finest, most upstanding citizens of our communities have been guilty of sexually abusing children. When we discover that judges, lawyers, doctors, school teachers, ministers, and priests are capable of molesting children, we find that we simply can't predict who will be a molester and who won't. There are, however, certain behaviors and personality characteristics that are common among men who sexually abuse children. These are warning signs, or red flags, that the person may be more likely to sexually abuse a child. These indicators should not be singled out but seen in their entirety, as a unit. Although not every molester will have every characteristic, if the person your loved one is claiming to be her molester has many of these characteristics, you will have one more reason to believe her:

1. Poor impulse control.
2. Low self-esteem.
3. Selfishness and narcissism.
4. Neediness and a tendency to make demands (on your time, attention, and so on).
5. Timidity, lack of assertiveness, feelings of inadequacy, social awkwardness, poor social skills, difficulty developing adult social and sexual relationships.
6. Alcohol abuse, alcoholism, and drug addiction.
7. History of being sexually abused as a child.
8. History of being abusive (physically, verbally, sexually) as an adult or older child.
9. History of mental illness.
10. Dependent personality (unable to support oneself financially or emotionally).
11. "Loves" to be with children, relates to children much better than adults, acts more like a child than an adult.

12. Antisocial behavior (does not believe in society's rules, has own set of rules that seem to accommodate his desires). Aggressive, abusive behavior.
13. Withdrawal into one's own world, an extremely active fantasy life.
14. Inability to have a successful relationship with an adult woman.
15. Overly sexed, preoccupied with sex, needs to have sex daily or several times a day, masturbates compulsively.
16. Does not seem to have any limits when it comes to sex—anything goes. Attracted to "kinky" sex such as discipline and bondage, sadomasochism. Overly involved in "alternative lifestyles" such as "wife swapping," nudity, sex clubs.
17. Overly involved in pornography: Constantly reads porno magazines, watches porno movies.
18. Exposure to and interest in pornography involving *children*.
19. Showing more interest in your children than in you. Many pedophiles marry a woman in order to have access to her children.
20. Attraction to satanism. There is a strong connection between white racism, satanism and child sex abuse.
21. Sexual repression, moralistic behavior, feeling guilty about sex (Catholic or Fundamentalist background).
22. Sexual impotency or other sexual dysfunction with adult females.
23. Need to feel powerful and controlling.

The majority of perpetrators are relatives, most notably, stepfathers, fathers, uncles, grandfathers, and older siblings, as well as mothers, grandmothers, and aunts. It has been estimated that 90 percent of child sexual abuse occurs in the home or at the hands of people known to the family. Although the majority of all victims were sexually abused within the family, boys are more likely than girls to be victimized by someone outside of the family.

In his book *Child Sexual Abuse: New Theory and Research*, David Finkelhor noted that having a stepfather constitutes one of the strongest risk factors, more than doubling a girl's chance of being sexually molested.

Moreover, his study revealed that a stepfather is five times more likely to sexually victimize a daughter than is a natural father.

While both women and gay men do sexually abuse children, the majority of all child molesters are heterosexual males who are usually young or middle-aged.

Based on my many years of working in the field of childhood sexual abuse, I have compiled some typical personality profiles that best describe the different types of child molesters.

1. THE "I'VE GOT TO HAVE IT—NOW!" PERSON.

This person has little or no control over his impulses and sets no limits to the fulfilment of his desires, whether they be for food, alcohol, sex, or material possessions. If he wants something, he wants it now, whether it is appropriate or not, whether the other person wants the same thing or not. If a person has this problem, he will be unable or unwilling to set *limits* on his behavior. He'll be unable to control when he will become sexual, for instance, and even where he will have sex. This kind of person is different from the norm in that he *acts* on his impulses whether they are socially acceptable or not. He will not *restrain* himself. His needs take precedence over other people's feelings or even society's rules. He may feel bad about it afterward, but he cannot control his urges until they are satisfied.

2. THE "I AM POWERLESS" PERSON.

This person has extremely low self-esteem and a low sense of efficacy (competence and power). He feels immature and inadequate, and because of his low self-esteem, he prefers partners who are younger, smaller, and weaker than himself. He may have few adult friends and may have had few if any adult sexual relationships. Because his psychological development is arrested, he may experience himself as a child, with childlike emotional needs. He may be attracted to a partner because she represents a nurturing parent—someone who will take care of him and protect him but make few sexual demands—or because she has children.

3. THE ANTISOCIAL PERSONALITY.

Antisocial personalities do not live by the same set of rules and values as most people. Instead, they have their own set of rules, rules that usually make little or no sense and that seem to be made with only their own desires in mind and that justify their antisocial acts. Often involved with illegal acts, gambling, pornography, sexual abuse, violence, and alcohol or drug abuse, they tend to blame others or to offer plausible rationalizations for their behavior. Grossly selfish, callous, irresponsible, impulsive, and unable to feel guilt or to learn from experience and punishment, they are self-serving and are masters at justifying even the cruelest actions.

Such people typically were severely physically, emotionally, or verbally—and possibly sexually—abused as children. Males brutalized by fathers often develop strong antisocial characteristics. (Their lack of respect for society's rules leads to a history of arrests, fighting, rebelling, alcoholism and drug abuse.)

They often attempt to control others through manipulation or aggression. They are often considered to be con artists, since they are so good at manipulating people in order to get their way. These are the people who will promise everything and deliver nothing but more promises. They are often incapable of significant loyalties to individuals, groups, or social values.

An antisocial male will lie without compunction, telling his mate he has paid the bills when instead he has gambled the money away or spent it on another woman. When confronted, he will lash out at his mate and make her feel sorry that she doubted him. Since his frustration tolerance is low, he is quick to anger and can be very explosive, thus discouraging any real confrontation.

4. THE "I CAN'T MAKE IT WITH A WOMAN" MAN.

Men who are unable to function sexually with an adult woman, either because of impotency problems or because they were sexually abused by a woman when they were a child and fear being intimate, will often gravitate to children to satisfy their sexual needs. They may feel humiliated because of their lack of potency and give up trying with an adult women. This does not mean that every man who has a sexual dysfunction will become a child molester, but those with sexual problems need psychotherapy or sex therapy in order to resolve the problem. Untreated, their sexual failure will increasingly whittle away at their self-esteem, making them more prone to seek sexual fulfillment in less conventional ways.

5. THE SEXUAL "CHILD."

This person does not act like an adult or does not want you to act like an adult when you have sex. Sex is an *adult* activity. Even though it is healthy to be in touch with our "inner child" and to feel our childlike emotions freely, acting like a child with our partner or being needy and babyish while having sex is seldom healthy. This does not mean we cannot be playful and spontaneous with sex, but we should still be in our adult mode most of the time during sexual activity. If your partner consistently wants to talk baby talk to you or otherwise acts like a child during sex, it may indicate that he was sexually abused as a child and is suffering from arrested development and sexual confusion. If he consistantly wants *you* to talk baby talk to him or to otherwise act like a child before or during sex, he might be getting off on imagining he is having sex with a child.

6. THE SEX ADDICT.

This person demands and pleads with you to have sex with him daily, or perhaps several times a day, and when you say no to him (because you are too tired, have to go to work, or are just not in the

44

mood), he becomes irate, hurt, or withdrawn. He may insist that he desires sex with you so much because he loves you so much, because he needs you so much, or because you turn him on, but the truth is his strong sexual drive has little or nothing to do with you or his feelings for you and may not even have anything to do with sex. He is using sex primarily as a release—a release of tension from a very demanding job, trouble with his boss, or other personal problems. He learned very early in childhood that sex could relieve his stress and reduce tension. He may have learned this by masturbating when he felt upset, angry, and hurt, or he may have been introduced to sex very early on (perhaps by an adult). Now, as an adult, whenever he is under pressure or unhappy about something, he may fall back on his old stand-by. The sexual release temporarily relaxes him and takes his mind off his problems. Since it is only a temporary physiological release and has not solved any life problems, the need to further reduce tension remains, and so does the demand for excessive sex.

Other sex addicts use sex as a way of temporarily feeling better about themselves or feeling powerful. Again, perhaps they learned while very young to masturbate as a way of comforting themselves, soothing themselves when they were in a frightening, uncomfortable, or stressful situation. Now, when they feel insecure or fearful, they may automatically seek sex as a refuge and solace. This in itself is not an unhealthy practice, just as it wasn't necessarily unhealthy when they were children to masturbate as a means of comfort. But the point here is that these people have made an *unusually*, often abnormally strong connection between sex and frustration. Whenever they are frustrated or feel bad about themselves, they want and need sex. If sex is not forthcoming, they become even more frustrated. By the same token, they may seek sex when they feel insecure and *powerless* as a way of feeling more in control and powerful. The habit or compulsion to have sex in order to feel powerful may very well have come from having been sexually abused as a child. They now rely on compulsive, inordinate sex to feel powerful and strong or to give vent to their rage at having been abused themselves.

To summarize, these individuals who are obsessed with and addicted to sex must have it nearly all the time or be engaged in some kind of sexually related activity. They constantly engage in "kinky" acts (such as tying you up or being tied up, flagellation or humiliation), pore through porno magazines, stay glued to the VCR watching X-rated movies, constantly want to explore alternative life-styles such as nudist colonies, swinger clubs, "wife-swapping," bisexuality, and sadomasochism. Sex has become an obsession, a compulsion, a way of pushing down feelings that keep trying to emerge but are allowed no healthy outlet or release. To them, sex is a convenient way of avoiding their feelings of insecurity, power-lessness, and rage—a quick fix that always wears off and demands another round. To these people, sex is not love, it is power, avoid-ance, and temporary reassurance.

Not all child molesters fall into one of these six categories, but if the accused perpetrator sounds like one of the people I've described, he definitely *is* capable of sexually abusing a child. This information, cou-pled with the other information I have provided, should help you to determine whether you should believe your relative or not.

The following chapters will address the concerns of each member of the family and discuss possible reasons why you might have an invest-ment in not believing the survivor.

4

HOW PARENTS COPE WITH THE NEWS

It hurts to learn that your son or daughter was sexually abused as a child. It hurts deep down inside—so deep, in fact, that you might not be able to find the hurt right away. The pain may be so intense that you can't allow yourself to feel it for a while. But it still hurts.

Don't be surprised if your initial response to this news is denial or anger. This is just your way of protecting yourself from the pain. You may accuse your child of lying even though somewhere inside you really believe her. You might get angry and say something like "Why didn't you ever tell me?" or "Why did you let it happen?" as an initial response because you are so shocked at the news. We've all learned to protect ourselves from the truth by getting angry at others, blaming others, or denying that what they are saying is true. But that doesn't mean that we don't know the truth. The following examples are typical of how parents react at first to this devastating information:

"I still remember the day my son told me that his uncle had sexually abused him when he was a child. My whole body went numb, and I just stood there looking at him for the longest time, saying nothing. And then the first thing out of my mouth was, 'Why didn't you come to me? Why didn't you tell me?' He tried to answer me, but I wasn't listening. I just kept accusing him of being a bad son instead of being there for him at a time when he needed me."

"When my daughter first told me that my father had molested her, I immediately called her a liar. I remember saying to her, 'How dare you accuse your grandfather of such a terrible thing! He's always been so good to all of us, especially you. Now he's a sweet old man who needs our love, and here you are making up vicious lies about him.'"

To Mothers (Including Stepmothers, Foster Mothers, and Other Female Caretakers)

Why didn't I realize it was happening?

Many mothers did in fact sense that something wasn't quite right in the family but did not allow themselves to think that it could have been incest. Other mothers suspected incest but doubted their own perceptions, convincing themselves that they were reading too much into an innocent situation or that they were imagining something that wasn't really happening.

Since you were probably the primary caretaker, you were responsible for the survivor's protection and welfare as a child. This fact carries with it a myriad of confusing feelings, compounded further if the offender is your spouse, your parent, or another of your children. Your loyalties may be confused, especially when you or other members of your family are operating out of denial. Your feelings of anger, love, grief, and guilt may be both confusing and overwhelming.

Even when the perpetrator is not a family member, you may still tend to agonize over the terrible reality of the abuse. Many parents ask themselves, "Where was I? How could this have happened to my child? Why didn't I know about it?" While these questions are indeed important to ask yourself, many parents become so stuck in their guilt and grief that they are unavailable to the survivor. Others become so overwhelmed with their own feelings that they become immobilized and thus cause the survivor to feel she must reach out to take care of her parent. These kinds of responses can recreate the family environment that was present when your child was growing up—a climate where the survivor felt compelled to take care of her parent's emotional needs.

Mothers in particular seem to be hurt when they discover that their child did not tell them about the abuse. They take it as a personal affront that their child did not trust them enough to tell them. Some children feel overly responsible for their mothers and do not want to upset them. This often occurs when their mother appears to be too weak, overburdened, sick, or powerless to take care of herself properly, much less her children, as was the case with these two survivors:

"My mother had eight other children, and my father beat her. I didn't want to add to her problems by telling her that my brother was molesting me. Besides, I knew she wouldn't do anything. My brother was already beginning to order her around and intimidate her just like my father did. I knew she was afraid of him just like she was my father."

"I protected my mother by not ever telling her. I thought it would kill her if I told her my father was molesting me. She was always so sick, I just didn't think she could take it, so I never let on."

Obviously, children should not have to protect their parents, it should be the other way around. Responding to a disclosure in any of these ways will tend to delay the recovery process for the survivor. The survivor needs to focus on personal healing, not on meeting the needs of other family members. In addition, sexual abuse carries with it such shame that many children do not tell their mother about it. In fact, most children blame themselves for the abuse, for several reasons: they feel they brought it upon themselves; they cannot bring themselves to face the fact that someone they love could hurt them so; they derived some sexual pleasure from it; they were with a person or in a place they were warned to stay away from; or the perpetrator has told them it is their fault ("You are so sexy," "You shouldn't have worn those shorts," "You made me angry," "Females are temptresses," "You wanted it"). Because they feel they are to blame, they are ashamed to tell anyone, even their parents. They feel like they got themselves into this mess and thus they must suffer alone.

As much as it hurts to realize that your child has been hurt so deeply, it hurts even more to be told that the person who caused so much pain to your child was someone you still care very deeply about. Diana Russell, in her study entitled *The Secret Trauma, Incest in the Lives of Girls and Women*, found that more support was given to those victims who were abused by a more distant relative that those who were victimized by a close relative. This was the case with Margaret:

"I felt so torn when my daughter told me that her grandfather had molested her. I wanted to believe her, because I couldn't think of any reason why she would lie about such a thing. But at the same time I couldn't believe that my father could have done such a horrible thing either. I love them both very much, and I felt like I was put in the horrible position of having to choose one over the other."

WHEN THE ACCUSED PERPETRATOR IS OR WAS YOUR HUSBAND OR BOYFRIEND

There are so many conflicting feelings that come up when your child tells you that your husband or lover sexually abused her. Even though you may feel horrible for your child and the hurt that she must have gone through, you will also feel terribly betrayed. After all, she is talking about the man you love, or have loved in the past. How could he have possibly betrayed your love and trust in such a way? You may even feel jealous, as if your daughter was a rival, as happened to Lucy:

"When my daughter first told me that Ted had molested her, I became enraged—with her, with him, with the whole situation. I had finally met a man I could love, after so many years of being alone, and now here was my daughter telling me that he had preferred her over me! I immediately accused her of seducing him—of enticing him by walking around with shorts on all the time, showing off her young, sexy body. I had visions of them together, doing things he and I had done, and I hated them both.

"I didn't see it the way it really was at all. I didn't see my daughter as an innocent victim but rather as a grown woman and a rival. It took me quite a long time to realize that she was only thirteen when it began, still an innocent child, really. I realize now that I didn't want to have to feel the pain of knowing that Ted was capable of such a thing because it meant that our relationship was over."

Following the disclosure of father-daughter incest, a mother usually goes through some or all of the following reactions:

1. She is *angry* at her daughter for not revealing the incest sooner and at her husband for doing this to her child and to her.
2. She feels *guilty* that she has failed to protect her child and that she has failed to satisfy her husband. She thinks it may be her fault that the incest has occurred.
3. She feels *betrayed* by her husband because he has been living a lie and a little by her daughter for having kept the relationship a secret.
4. She *hates* her husband for the consequences of what he has done— the damage to the child, to *her* relationship with her own child, to the relationship between herself and her husband. He is the cause of all the difficulty everyone is now experiencing.
5. She is *repulsed* by him, keeps thinking about him touching her child and trying to get the thoughts out of her mind. How could he do it?
6. Sometimes she even feels a little *jealous* toward her daughter for the extra attention and special relationship that she seemed to have with her husband.
7. She is *confused*, because on the one hand she wants to support and help her child, but on the other hand you don't just change your feelings for someone even when you learn about sexual

abuse. New feelings are competing with the old ones. She feels caught between two sets of feelings, not sure what is best.

8. Most of all she feels that not only has she *failed* as a wife and mother but she is now *expected to take charge* of resolving all the problems that have resulted from the incest, even though she was not directly involved with the abuse or perhaps didn't even know about it at all.

The parent who has already ended the relationship with the perpetrator or has decided to leave the relationship will undoubtedly have the easiest time believing her child's accusations. She has less to lose, and her pride will not be as hurt. In fact, sometimes learning of the abuse can be the catalyst to end a bad relationship.

But the parent who wants to remain in the relationship with his or her husband or lover will have the hardest time believing her child. Some mothers find it almost impossible to believe their child because if they believe that their husband or lover has abused their child, it forces them to make choices and take some action, such as leaving the man they love, reporting him to the police, telling other family members in order to protect other children. On the other hand, if they don't believe their child, they will not be forced to take such actions, actions they are unable or unwilling to take at this time. It is far easier to deny that it ever happened, to convince themselves that their child is lying, making it up, or exaggerating.

TO FATHERS (INCLUDING STEPFATHERS, FOSTER FATHERS, AND OTHER MALE CARETAKERS)

Fathers have many of the same problems as mothers when they hear that their child was sexually abused. Like mothers, they will feel angry, guilty, betrayed, and sad. They will have a difficult time believing that the abuse occurred, especially if it was a relative or someone else they trusted and cared about, and they will blame themselves for not protecting their child. But in addition to these shared reactions, fathers have some reactions that are unique to them.

WHEN IT WAS YOUR DAUGHTER WHO WAS SEXUALLY ABUSED

Many fathers feel very possessive of their daughters. When a possessive father discovers that his daughter has been molested, he may become so enraged with the perpetrator that he is unable to give his daughter the emotional support she needs. He may become so obsessed with revenge that he doesn't focus on the task at hand—listening to his daughter, letting her know he believes her, and being as supportive as he can be. In fact, many survivors are afraid of what their fathers might do when they're told about the abuse, as was the case with Melissa:

"I was afraid to tell my father that his best friend Tom had sexually abused me because I was afraid my father would kill him. I never told him when I was a child, but as an adult I decided to tell him in order to facilitate my recovery. Just as I had feared, he became enraged and stormed out the door looking for Tom, leaving me sitting there all alone with my pain. Not only was I all alone but I had to worry about what he was going to do."

Fathers, even more than mothers, can blame themselves for not protecting their daughters. Viewing their female children as weak and vulnerable, fathers take on the role of protector and guardian. When harm comes to a daughter, especially sexual abuse, the father sees himself as a failure. This is how Andrea's father reacted when she told him that she had been abused by a neighbor:

"My father never forgave himself for my being molested. He always said that if he had protected me better it wouldn't have happened. But I don't know how he could have prevented it without locking me in the house night and day, which I think he would have liked to do. He was always so overprotective anyway, never letting me spend the night with my friends, not letting me go on camping trips or field trips at school. He couldn't have known that I would be abused by someone in my own neighborhood. The only thing I blame my dad for is that I didn't feel I could come to him and tell him about it. I was too worried about getting in trouble, too afraid he might blame me."

Many fathers become angry with their daughters for not telling them about the sexual abuse. But daughters seldom tell their mothers they were abused, much less their fathers. In fact, those children who are able to tell their mothers sometimes beg them not to tell their fathers. They, like the clients above, are either afraid of what their father will do to the perpetrator, or are afraid of being blamed by their father for being in the wrong place at the wrong time, for not fighting back, and so on.

All too often, fathers place too much importance on their daughters' virginity and on their remaining "Daddy's little girl." Because of this, a daughter may be too embarrassed to tell her father and feel that she has somehow let him down, that she is now tainted and spoiled.

Some fathers are so pained by the news that a daughter was abused that they can barely be around her or look her in the eye for fear of seeing her pain. Unfortunately, this kind of behavior on a father's part can be misinterpreted as his being ashamed of his daughter.

When Your Daughter Was Abused by a Female

As I have mentioned before, perpetrators of childhood sexual abuse are not always male. If your daughter was sexually abused by her mother, her sister, her grandmother, her aunt, or any other female, this disclosure will probably be not only painful and shocking to you but also embarrassing. Males in general and fathers in particular don't quite know what to do with the whole issue of sex between females. They are embarrassed by it, but also often a little bit aroused by the idea. It will make the entire issue a lot easier for you if you remember that child sexual abuse is not really about sex at all. It is about power—one person's having power over another, one person's taking control over another. While we don't tend to think of females as the perpetrators of violent crimes such as physical abuse or rape, they are indeed just as capable of such acts. Your daughter was just as violated, just as damaged by a female perpetrator as she would have been by a male.

If your daughter was sexually abused by her mother or stepmother, she was particularly damaged. The special bond between mother and child is by far the most important human bond that can occur. When that bond is confused by sexuality, the resulting damage can render a child permanently scarred. When a child cannot trust her own mother, she will find it difficult ever to trust anyone again. Your daughter will need your support now more than ever, because she must know that she still has one parent she can turn to.

WHEN IT WAS YOUR SON WHO WAS SEXUALLY ABUSED

Many fathers, upon hearing that their son was sexually abused, make the same mistake that much of society does: they assume that their son should have been able to defend himself. Because we as a society have a difficult time recognizing that a male can be just as vulnerable as a female, you may be ashamed of your son for not "fighting back," for being passive rather than aggressive. This may be particularly true if the perpetrator was a female. After all, you may reason, a female cannot exactly *force* a male to have sex.

This kind of reasoning couldn't be further from the truth. An adult female can easily overpower a male child and forcibly fondle him, perform oral sex, or insert fingers or instruments into his anus. A female perpetrator can also seduce a male child into doing things that he really doesn't want to do by exposing herself to him, caressing him, or kissing him. The boy, because he is so easily aroused, may go along with the female's seductiveness even though he feels fearful, guilty, or ashamed.

When Rodney was 12 years old, his older sister Samantha would lock him in the bathroom. She would press her body against his, fondle his genitals and kiss him until he became extremely aroused. Even though he tried to fight her off, he was no match for his sister, who was four years older than he and much stronger. He would eventually give in and allow her to masturbate him to orgasm, but he would feel horrible about himself afterward.

"I felt so humiliated each time it happened," he recalls. "I didn't want my sister to touch me like that, but it was like my body just took over. I hated it, and I hated myself for letting it happen. I felt like such a wimp, such a pansy. And I felt so horribly guilty for letting my own sister touch me. I felt like such a pervert."

There is much more involved in the sexual abuse of male children than physical strength. A male child faces a particular form of confusion and isolation when he is sexually abused by a female. Males who are sexually abused by a female tend to feel an added level of shame. They are more likely to blame themselves or to tell themselve that what happened was not really abuse.

This is especially true when the perpetrator is the survivor's mother. Mothers occupy a special, almost sacred place in our culture. For many people it is unthinkable that a mother would not be a nurturing, protective, loving figure. Even children who have experienced extreme forms of physical, emotional, and sexual abuse at the hands of their mothers may find themselves protecting their tormentors through self-blame and pretense.

It can be even harder for a father to picture his son being completely overpowered by another male, or to recognize that an abuser could "outsmart" his son and manipulate him into doing things he really didn't want to do. He may secretly believe that his son is a sissy or, worse yet, a homosexual—otherwise why did he attract another male's attention in the first place? He may even accuse his son of being gay, thus adding to his son's victimization. Whether his son is gay or not, the insinuation is the same—the abuse was his fault, and he was not man enough to fight back. If his son is not gay, his father's accusations may make him doubt his sexual orientation. And if he is gay, he may blame himself even more for the sexual abuse.

If you are plagued by the question of why the perpetrator picked your son, it is important for you to know that those who molest children pick whoever is available. If it hadn't been your son, it would have been whoever else was in close proximity. While there is some evidence to show that children who are neglected or improperly supervised are molested more often than children whose parents provide them with adequate supervision, we also know that molesters are extremely clever people who are able to fool adults as well as children into believing that they are trustworthy, caring people. Many male children are sexually abused by coaches, camp counselors, and baby-sitters—people who are supposed to care deeply for children.

To repeat, the vast majority of all child molesters are heterosexual males, although both women and gay men may also sexually abuse children. If it seems contradictory that a heterosexual male would molest a male child, it is probably because you think of sexual abuse as a sexual act. But experts in the field of child abuse have come to realize that it is not a sexual act but an act of violence. A child molester is using his or her power and authority as a weapon against a child's vulnerability and innocence. In much the same way that a rapist violates his female victim out of anger toward women, a child molester violates a child out of anger toward innocence—often avenging the lost innocence of his own childhood.

It will naturally be very difficult for you to face the fact that your son was victimized. But victimized he was. He didn't invite the advances. He didn't encourage the abuser. And he was not in any way responsible for what happened. A young boy is no match for an adult of either sex, and children are easily manipulated and controlled by adults, especially those they care about and those who have authority over them.

TO BOTH PARENTS

In this section I discuss the feelings and issues that you will be dealing with, depending upon who the perpetrator was.

WHEN THE PERPETRATOR IS YOUR PARENT

As hard as it is to believe that your spouse or lover could have sexually abused your child, it is even harder to believe that your own parent could do such a thing. How can someone accept the fact that his or her father or mother is a child molester? Those parents who have a good relationship with their father or mother will have an especially difficult time believing their child, because what their child is telling them doesn't match their image of their parent. This was Teresa's experience:

"When my son told me that his grandfather, my father, had sexually abused him, I felt like my head had left my body. I could still hear him talk, I could still see his face, but I couldn't feel my body at all. I had no reason to believe that my son would lie about such a thing, but it was incomprehensible to me that my own father could have ever done what he was saying he did to him. My father was a wonderful man, and I loved him dearly. I would never imagine him hurting anyone, much less my son."

Even those who don't get along well with their parent or who recognize that their parent has problems still find it difficult to believe he would do this kind of thing, as Dan did:

"My father was no saint. He was a liar, a womanizer, and a drunk. But he adored children, and I couldn't picture him ever deliberately hurting one. He'd always been good to me—he never beat me or even yelled at me, and I assure you he never laid a hand on me. I just couldn't believe my son, no matter how hard I tried."

Surprisingly, even those who were themselves sexually abused by the accused parent will still have a difficult time coming to terms with the news that the same thing happened to their own child. Karen had the following reaction:

"I always felt that the reason my father became sexual with me was because we had a special relationship. He always told me that he wished things were different and that I had been his wife instead of his daughter. Hearing my daughter tell me that he said the same things to her, that he did the same things to her, made me realize that I had been fooling myself all along. I never really got angry at my father, because I loved him so much, and I felt sorry for him. But now I was seeing him differently, not as a loving man but as a manipulative one, not as a good father but as a user. It was one of the most difficult things I have ever had to do to give up my illusions about my father."

Because we know that child sexual abuse gets passed down from one generation to another, if your parent sexually abused you it is highly probable that he continued this behavior with your children. It is also likely that your parent was sexually abused himself by someone in his family and that if your child does not get professional help and the support from you that she needs, that she will continue the cycle of abuse with her children. You have a chance to break this cycle of abuse by believing your child and by getting professional help yourself for the damage the abuse by your father or mother caused you.

Many parents have completely blocked out any memory of having been sexually abused by their own father or mother. Sometimes this is because they were abused at a very early age, even in their infancy. Sometimes it is because they felt so betrayed that their own parent would do such a thing to them. And sometimes it is because the abuse was so violent, so sinister, that they couldn't tolerate the emotional and physical pain and so needed to block it out. Pay attention to how your body reacts when your child tells you about the abuse by your parent. Even though you may not have any conscious memory of the abuse, your body may remind you of it. As I mentioned earlier, our bodies have what is called "body memories," memories that are stored in the musculature of our bodies. It is very common for victims of sexual abuse to experience feelings in their bodies that are actually reminders of their own abuse.

For example, since your child has told you about being sexually abused, have you felt tingling or pain in your vagina, penis, or anus? Have you had to urinate frequently? Or have you had more general symptoms, such as dizziness, nausea, or a tightness in your stomach, chest, or jaw? These may all be indications that you were sexually abused as a child, perhaps by the same perpetrator who abused your child.

Have you had nightmares or dreams involving you and your parent? Or have scenes flashed through your head in which you see your parent abusing you? These may be flashbacks of actual events.

WHEN THE PERPETRATOR WAS YOUR MOTHER

As I mentioned earlier, there are far more female sex abusers than one might think. It is not unheard of for a mother to sexually abuse her own children and for sisters to abuse their siblings. Even grandmothers have been known to sexually abuse their grandchildren.

Facing the fact that your mother sexually abused one of your children is heartbreaking. Not only will you experience all the pain that any parent feels when she discovers her child has been abused, but you will have to face the almost unbearable pain of losing your own mother. No matter what the outcome, whether you choose to continue a relationship with your mother or not, your relationship with her will be permanently changed. You will no longer view her in the same way, you will no longer feel the same about her, and you will no longer relate to her as you did.

The thing that will most help you believe your child and cope with the painful information is to remind yourself that your mother was most certainly sexually abused herself as a child and was therefore reenacting her own abuse with your child. This reminder will not make the pain go away, nor will it necessarily reduce your anger toward her, but it will make sense of a seemingly senseless act of betrayal and cruelty.

Unfortunately, along with the relief this reminder tends to bring, it also opens up a whole new can of worms. If your mother was reenacting her own abuse with your child, the chances are extremely high that she did the same with you and/or your siblings. Victims of sexual abuse who are prone to reenact their own abuse seldom if ever skip a generation or begin to abuse late in life. Being sexually abused by your own mother may have been so excruciatingly painful and shame-inducing that you repressed the memory entirely. However, now that your child is telling you about her abuse at the hands of your mother, your denial system may begin to break down and your own memories begin to surface. If this is the case, you will need to seek professional help immediately, for your own recovery as well as the recovery of your child. If you do not get into psychotherapy yourself, you will probably begin to doubt your own memories or push them back down, and in turn, may refuse to believe your child. As difficult as it is to face the pain of such a betrayal by your own parent, you do not want to turn your back on your child and thus betray her trust.

WHEN THE PERPETRATOR WAS YOUR SIBLING

If you know for a fact that your sibling sexually abused you, then you have every reason to believe your child when she tells you that he also abused her. If you have a vague memory or a nagging feeling that perhaps your sibling may have abused you, now you have proof that he did. And if you thought that you and your brother or sister were both responsible for the incest between you, you now need to update your thinking.

Remember, even if your brother or sister was only a few years older than you, he or she had more personal power, more strength, and more experience than you. You were not responsible but were instead coerced, threatened, or bribed into doing something you were not equipped to handle yet. He or she damaged your self-esteem, caused you to feel a tremendous amount of shame and guilt for something you had no control over, caused you to distance yourself from your parents, sexualized you too early on, and took away your opportunity to choose your first sexual partner. And this is exactly what your sibling has now done to your child. Your loyalties need to be with your child now, against the very same person who damaged you.

If you have no memories of being sexually abused by your sibling, it doesn't necessarily mean that such abuse didn't occur. It may be that you have blocked out the memory in order to protect yourself from the pain of feeling the betrayal and fear associated with the experience. It will help both you and your child if you seek professional help in order to explore the possibility. If you are not willing to do this, then perhaps you might be willing to talk to your other siblings and ask them if the accused sibling ever sexually abused them when they were children. In addition, it will be vitally important for you to talk to your other children, your nieces and nephews, and any other children who have been around the accused sibling, to find out if anyone else in the family has been sexually abused by the same person. Again, the chances are very high that your child is not the only victim in your family.

Although it will be very difficult to ask other family members and to risk getting them upset with you, you need to be willing to do anything in order to expose the abuse in your family. In addition, your child will feel very supported by you for being willing to seek the truth and to work on this family problem. A word of caution is in order, however. Just because no one else in the family admits to having been sexually abused by your sibling does not mean that he did not in fact abuse others in the family. Remember that most people either hide the fact that they were sexually abused, out of fear or shame, or have no memories of the abuse. But even if this is the case in your family, at the very least you have taken the first step by exposing the truth and making everyone in the family aware of the problem.

Your family needs to understand that your sibling needs help so that he does not continue to sexually abuse children, either inside or outside of the family. If the situation is handled as a family problem, which in fact it is, the entire family could work together to ensure that your sibling gets some help or that he never has access to children again.

WHEN THE PERPETRATOR WAS ANOTHER ONE OF YOUR CHILDREN

"When my daughter told me that her brother had sexually abused her when she was a child, I was shocked. I couldn't imagine what she was talking about. Whenever I had thought of sexual abuse I had always imagined an adult abusing a child. But a child abusing a child? That didn't make sense. Her brother was only a few years older than she. How could he have *forced* her to do anything? And why didn't she tell me about it?"

This is a common reaction to being told by one of your children that her sibling sexually abused her. As mentioned in chapter 1, few people understand that sibling incest can indeed be the sexual abuse of one child by another. The average parent doesn't want to know that her children have been sexual with one another in the first place, much less that one child forced the other into it. As one mother put it, "How can I face the fact that one of my children was being held captive by another of my children in my own home?"

Few parents can face even the possibility of sibling sexual abuse without blaming the victimized child. Like many parents in this situation, you may have a difficult time believing that your child didn't feel safe or close enough to you to come to you and tell you if she felt threatened. You probably can't believe that something like this could go on right under your nose without your realizing it. You may feel betrayed by both children, almost as if both children conspired to get away with something behind your back.

Often, the victim is blamed in cases of sexual abuse between siblings, particularly between an older brother and a younger sister. When a victim is blamed for the sexual abuse, she is in essence revictimized. This was the case with Carla:

"One night my father walked in on my brother and me. Much to my surprise, he just turned around and walked out without saying anything to us. The next morning, though, he insisted that I go to confession. Nothing was said to my brother, and so consequently he continued. I knew if I tried to tell my parents they would blame me, so I just kept quiet. My father never treated me the same after that. He treated me like I was a bad person, as if I was the one who had done something wrong."

Instead of blaming the victim, you need to educate yourself concerning sibling sexual abuse.

Older siblings who have been violated themselves are often capable of being extremely violent toward younger siblings. Many victims of sibling abuse were terrorized by older siblings who threatened them with violence or who forcibly raped or sodomized them. In general, the greater the age difference, the greater the betrayal of trust and the more violent the incest tends to be. In some cases of older brother–younger sister abuse, there is tremendous violence, with the brother using immense force.

"My brother began by getting in bed with me at night and rubbing up against me with his penis. I knew he shouldn't be doing this, but I liked having him in bed with me because I felt so alone in our family. Before long, he was fondling me, which eventually progressed to sexual intercourse over the next several years. When I was 12 years old, I started to physically resist my brother. This made him angry, and he began to violently rape me, both in the vagina and in the anus."

When a brother or sister is much older than his or her younger sibling (five years or more), the younger sibling may see the older as a parental figure. Thus, the sense of betrayal can be almost as great as that experienced by a child when her parent betrays trust by crossing the line.

Some older siblings will use trickery to get what they want, such as telling their younger sibling they are going to teach them about sex. At other times, an older sibling uses threats in order to make a younger sibling comply, as in the following case:

"My older brother was always hitting me and pushing me, so I was already afraid of him even before he started molesting me. If I tried to resist, he would hit me or threaten to hit me. After it was over, he'd threaten to kill me if I told anyone about it. I'd seen what he was capable of when he was angry, because one time I saw him kill a cat."

More than almost any other kind of abuse, sibling abuse causes the victim to feel tremendously guilty. Because there isn't as clear a distinction as there is when an adult is the perpetrator, many younger siblings feel as responsible for the incidents as the older one, especially if there was any sexual pleasure involved, as there was with Tracey:

"Although I felt terrorized each time my brother entered my room, I eventually began to respond to his touch. The only time he was gentle or affectionate with me was when he was being sexual with me, and I was hungry for some affection. The abuse continued for six more years, until I was old enough to move out of the house."

Because they responded to the touches and felt pleasure, and often because the incest continued for many years, many victims become convinced that they wanted it, that they were bad or evil, and sometimes even that they were the instigator. As time goes by, they become even more confused as to exactly what went on, particularly if the older sibling blames them for the incest, as it was with Kendra:

"My brother always told me that I was an evil seductress, that I made him feel the way he did because of the way I dressed and the way I walked. I didn't know what he meant, because I always tried to cover my body as completely as possible and not to walk in a sexy way. After he would have a climax he would always look at me with disgust and say, 'Look what you made me do!' I never understood, because he would be the one to come to my room at night, but I did begin to feel aroused after a while, so I guess he was right."

In most cases, sibling sexual abuse is accompanied by physical and emotional abuse. The sexual assaults usually continue in a compulsive manner until the abused child is old enough to forcibly prohibit the behavior, the behavior is discovered and stopped, or the victim is old enough to leave home.

In cases of sibling abuse, parents' loyalties to both children are in conflict. It is hard enough for a parent to have to choose between a spouse and a child, but what if it comes down to a choice between one child and another? Whether they realize it or not, many parents take the side of the accused child, and by doing so, sever the bond between themselves and the victimized child. Even in cases where the parent refuses to take sides, the victimized child often ends up being disbelieved and unsupported, as was the case with Sydney:

"I still remember the day my daughter told me about the incest between herself and her brother. She told me that she was in therapy because it had damaged her so much. I just couldn't understand what all the fuss was about. After all, they were both kids. I know that what they did was wrong, but I blame both of them. They both will have to answer to God for doing the unspeakable. My daughter is angry with me now and is threatening never to see me again if I don't stop seeing my son. How can she ask this of me? How can I turn my back on my own flesh and blood? I was taught to forgive and forget, and I have forgiven both of them. I just pray to God that he forgives them."

As was the case with the mother and daughter above, it is not uncommon for the abused child to demand that her parent(s) not only acknowledge that she was abused but also stop seeing the offending sibling. As painful as this can be to you as a mother or father, it is important that you try to understand why your child is demanding these things from you.

First of all, as I mentioned in chapter 1, most sibling incest is indeed abuse because one sibling coerces, threatens, or bribes the other into doing his bidding sexually, while the younger sibling goes along with or puts up with acts that she really doesn't want to be involved with.

Most victims of sibling abuse feel as betrayed by their parents as they do by the abusive sibling. They cannot understand why their parents didn't notice their symptoms, why they didn't protect them from the abusive sibling, and most important, why their parents don't believe them now. More than anything, they want their parents to understand their pain and to stand up for them now against the abusive sibling.

Because you didn't protect them from the abuse then, because you didn't recognize the abuse and stop it, they need you to take their side now. They need you as their parent to do now what you couldn't do then — to stand up to their abuser and tell him that what he did was wrong.

If you cannot do this, your child will continue to feel betrayed by you. She will continue to feel that you have chosen your other child over her, that you refuse to recognize how much damage he caused her.

WHY DIDN'T I KNOW IT WAS GOING ON?

Most parents are not on the lookout for sexuality between their children, much less sexual abuse. They assume that their children will observe the incest taboo and that their older children will feel protective of their younger siblings. This was Lynn's experience:

"Looking back on it, I realize that I was being incredibly naive. My son seemed very possessive of his younger sister, but I assumed it was because he was feeling like a typical older brother. I never imagined he felt sexual toward her, and I certainly never imagined he was molesting her. She seemed to adore him, so I thought nothing of it when they would spend time together, even though I realize now that a normal boy his age wouldn't want to spend so much time with his younger sister. He should have been out with kids his own age.

"I realize now that he had never gone out with girls his age but always with girls who were much younger than himself. His wife is 10 years younger than he is. My daughter says that he married her because she is so childlike, and I guess I can see what she means. I guess he does have a real problem. My daughter is afraid he is molesting his own daughter."

Sometimes parents are blind to a son's abusive ways because they themselves grew up in an environment where males were given preferential treatment and females were treated like second-class citizens. When they have their own children, they pass on this misogynistic legacy, as was the case with Suzanne, a client of mine:

"My mother always preferred my brothers over me. I was taught to wait on my father and my brothers and to always do as they said. My mother basically ignored me, except to depend on me to help her with the chores. My oldest brother was always a bully with me, hitting me, yelling at me, making me do whatever he wanted. When I complained to my mother about him, she would just accuse me of being rebellious and of making a big deal out of nothing. Then he started coming into my room at night after everyone was asleep and touching my body. The first time it happened I tried to stop him, but he held me down and told me that if I made any sounds he would kill me. He really scared me, and I believed he was capable of doing most anything to get his way.

After that, he came into my room every night and did whatever he wanted to me. I was afraid of him, but I also knew my mother would never believe me and would take his side if I did try to tell her."

And of course, some parents cannot recognize even the most obvious signs of sexual abuse because they themselves were sexually abused as children and are in deep denial about their own feelings. Rita, who had been sexually abused by both her father and her older brother, was completely blinded to her own daughter's symptoms and pleas for help when her older brother began to abuse her. Having blocked out the memory of her own abuse, Rita could not recognize her daughter's symptoms without having to face the pain of her own long-buried secret.

As with Rita, you may have been sexually abused yourself and have no conscious memory of it. If you have *any* reason to believe this might be the case, seek professional help or join a support group for survivors of sexual abuse. Groups are especially good for those who don't have clear memories, because hearing others' stories sometimes jogs their own memories.

WHY DID MY CHILD DO IT?

Whatever happens between siblings is a reflection of what is going on in the family in general, whether it is rivalry, overdepence, or abuse. Often, children who do not get what they need from their parents will turn to one another. Thus, a younger sibling will often look to an older one for the nurturing and guidance withheld by her parents. This gives the older sibling far too much influence and power over the younger one. By the same token, anger that cannot be expressed toward parents is often acted out on one's sibling.

Parental attitudes toward the opposite sex can also create an environment that is conducive to sibling abuse. For example, if both father and mother are misogynistic—that is, if they both distrust, dislike, and disregard females and view them as inferior to males—this attitude will obviously be passed down to their children. Male children will be given preferential treatment, and female children will be regarded as inferior to the males in the household. This kind of attitude gives the message to the males that they can demand subservience from their sisters and that they can do whatever they want to them. Since females are not respected, they know that their word will be honored over their sister's, and thus they do not fear punishment.

Males who sexually abuse their younger sisters do so for other reasons as well. Some have been given silent permission to act in this way by observing the way the family functions. A boy who has seen his father emotionally, physically, or sexually abuse his mother gets the message that it is okay to be abusive to females. A boy who discovers that his father is sexually abusing his sister feels that he has the right to do the same. And mothers who allow their husbands or lovers to abuse them also give the message to their male children that it is okay to dominate and abuse females.

In addition to these family dynamics, children and teenagers become sexual abusers because they were sexually abused themselves, by someone inside or outside the family. Sexualized too early, full of anger and self-loathing, these victims often lash out at the weakest, most convenient person they can find—someone they know cannot or will not defend herself. More males than females tend to identify with their aggressors, meaning they become like the person who abuses them as a way of coping with their pain and anger. But female children who have been abused can also reenact their own abuse by wielding power over a younger, weaker sibling.

DO I REALLY HAVE TO CHOOSE ONE CHILD OVER THE OTHER?

Of course, you don't want to have to choose one child over another, and you don't really have to do that if you are willing to stand up for what is right. It is not right to allow childhood sexual abuse to occur, and it certainly is not right to let it go unnoticed. Your son had no right to sexually abuse your daughter, no matter what his reasons were. And it is very possible that he is continuing his abusive behavior with his own children, his nieces and nephews, or any other children he has come in contact with. You need to take a stand against what he did then and confront him about the likelihood that he may still be sexually abusing children.

Some adult children who sexually abused their sibling(s) feel a great deal of remorse for what they did. Molesting their sibling has haunted them, making them feel guilty, ashamed, and evil. Although they cannot bring themselves to apologize to their sibling for the damage they inflicted, these adult children are often relieved when the truth is exposed once and for all.

If your child sexually molested a sibling, you will be doing him a great service by confronting him about the abuse. He has been burdened by his guilt for a long time, and you will do much to relieve him of it by letting him know you know. Then and only then will your child have the chance to get the help he most certainly needs. If he was sexually abused as a child, he was a victim too and needs professional assistance to help his wounds heal. If he received the message in the family that it was okay to abuse females, you will be doing a lot to change that message by letting him know now that it is *not* okay.

Unfortunately, most abusers do not admit the abuse, and your child may be no exception. Many perpetrators are incapable of feeling guilt or remorse or empathy for their victims. If this is the case with your child, he needs to at least know that you believe your other child, and that you are on to him. He needs to know that you suspect he is still molesting children and that you are watching him carefully.

If your child is a full-fledged child molester, he will probably not admit the abuse of his sibling. He has too much to lose. If you have any reason to believe that your child is such a person, you need to protect your grandchildren and any other children who may be around him from being molested by him. This includes reporting him to the authorities.

You aren't helping your child by protecting him. You are merely allowing him to continue his abusive behavior. While you will probably always love him, that doesn't mean you have to turn your back on your other child or on other potential victims. While you may feel sorry for the perpetrator and realize that he does indeed have a problem, you must hold him accountable for his behavior. He is the one who must reach out for help, and he will never do this as long as you protect him and make it possible for him to hide from the truth.

You really aren't choosing one child over another, but you are choosing to stop the cycle of abuse in your family. One adult child does not accuse another of sexually abusing her as a child unless there is truth to her accusation. Therefore, you are not only turning your back on the child who is making the accusation but also on the one who is accused if you refuse to take the accusation seriously, do some further investigating, and get professional help for the entire family. Sibling abuse occurs primarily in dysfunctional families and families where there is already a pattern of sexual abuse. The accused child may have been acting out family difficulties or may have been emotionally, physically, or sexually abused himself and therefore needs help to recover from such abuse. The entire family will need to learn healthier ways of interacting and communicating so that this kind of abuse does not continue to occur in the family.

Learning that your child was sexually abused as a child and that you were not only unable to stop it but unable to comfort her while she was going through this trauma has got to be one of the worst things a parent will ever have to deal with.

Hearing that your child was sexually abused can trigger an overwhelming variety of feelings. Anger, pain, guilt, and shame may all be mixed up together. Learning to fully accept the fact that the incest occurred and learning to cope with the changes that will inevitably result from it are processes that take time.

5

HOW SIBLINGS COPE WITH THE NEWS

When a sibling tells you that she was sexually abused as a child, it is of course a great shock. You will experience a mixture of feelings, depending upon who molested her. If it is someone you do not know, your feelings may mainly be anger and sadness that she was violated. But if she tells you that someone you care about sexually abused her, your initial reaction may be denial. You may find that you have much more of an investment in protecting your image of the perpetrator than you do in being there for your sibling. It is natural for you not to want to believe that a parent, grandparent, or another sibling could have done such a horrible thing.

But since people seldom make up this kind of story, since few people would voluntarily choose to identify themselves as a victim of childhood sexual abuse and even fewer would ever want to believe that someone they care about could hurt them so deeply, the chances are extremely high that your sibling is telling you the truth. If you care about your sibling, and even more important, if you care about yourself, it will behoove you to try to open up your mind and your heart to the strong possibility that she is telling you the truth.

If your sibling was sexually abused by a relative, it is very possible that you were abused by the same person. Statistics show that sexually abusive parents, siblings, grandparents, and uncles tend to victimize more than one child in the family. Sexually abusive fathers often begin molesting the oldest child in the family and gradually, as each child reaches a certain age, molest each child in the family. Grandparents, uncles, and aunts often molest all the children in the family. And sexually abusive siblings will often molest more than one sibling in the family. Since many children cope with abuse by blocking it out of their mind, it is possible that you have been sexually abused yourself but have not recovered the memories. Even if you are positive now that you were not also abused, you may discover that you completely change your mind later on as memories start to surface.

One of the ways to tell whether you may have also been abused by the same perpetrator is to notice how you have reacted to your sibling's telling you about her abuse. If you find yourself particularly anxious, upset, or angry when your sibling talks about the abuse, if you have pain or tingling in your genitals, or if you have been strongly resisting believing that she is telling the truth, be open to the possibility that it may also have happened to you. While it is natural to have a period of shock followed by difficulty adjusting to the idea, if you find that you are totally closed to the possibility, you may want to question why this is.

Christine didn't believe her sister Terry when she told her their father had molested her. "I realize now that I didn't want to believe her because I didn't want to face the fact that he had abused me too. I fought believing her for the longest time, telling myself that she was just trying to hurt my dad because they didn't get along, or that she was just trying to get attention. But gradually it began to sink in. Why would she say it was true if it wasn't? What possible reason could she have to make up such a horrible lie? I could see she was in pain, and I knew she was in therapy. Finally, I began to open up to the possibility that maybe she was telling the truth. I started asking her questions, started listening to her more, and finally I began to believe her. It wasn't too long after that that I remembered he had abused me also."

Many victims of childhood sexual abuse have completely forgotten the violation as a way of coping. Because you may have so far been able to block out your own abuse, your sibling is now a threat to you. She is bringing it all up again, reminding you of what it was like in your family, bringing up incidents you would prefer stay buried. For this reason, you may become extremely angry with her and even feel an unexplainable hatred for her.

Even if it turns out that you were not sexually abused, it will be important for you to realize that you have also been affected by the same family dynamics as your sibling. Because you probably both come from a dysfunctional family system, you, too, grew up in a family in which there was secrecy, pain, fear, and betrayal. You have also been betrayed by the perpetrator, because in order to abuse a child, a perpetrator must lie to everyone around him.

Even if the perpetrator didn't molest you, there are many other reasons why you don't want to believe your sibling. Many siblings knew that the abuse was going on but were helpless to prevent it. This sense of helplessness can cause deep scars, making you feel tremendously guilty, ashamed or inadequate, as Richard did:

"I knew my dad was molesting my sister, but I couldn't do anything about it. I wanted to stand up to him and tell him to stop, but I was afraid he'd beat me. I hated myself for years for being a coward, for not being a man."

Other siblings feel terrible guilt and shame because they were secretly glad the abuse was happening to their sibling and not themselves. This is what Diana told me in one of our counseling sessions:

"I slept in the same room with my sister, and night after night I would hear my dad's footsteps as he walked down the hall toward our room. My heart would be pounding, thinking that this was the night when he was going to come to my bed instead of hers. But every night he walked over to her bed, and I would breathe a sigh of relief that it wasn't me. Do you know how awful it is to feel like that? To know that you are such a creep that you actually want your sister to be hurt like that?"

It is hard to face these feelings of guilt, shame, and inadequency, and this is another reason why so many siblings deny the sexual abuse. They don't want to be reminded that they knew but could not help. They don't want to feel the guilt of being glad it was not they.

Some siblings feel tremendous jealousy toward the sibling who was being abused. Because they may not have known what was actually going on, they resented the amount of time and attention the perpetrator spent with the other sibling. This was the case with Carrie:

"For years I resented my older sister Janet. She was my father's favorite. He took her everywhere with him, bought her pretty dresses, and even bought her a car when she was 16. When she told me recently that our father had been having sex with her all along, I figured she deserved it. After all, she got all the attention I never got. I was glad she was hurt, glad she had suffered. Now, of course, I see it differently, but that was my initial reaction."

Other siblings are still so afraid of the perpetrator that they refuse to acknowledge what he did, even though they know it is true. Says one survivor: "When I told my sister Lynn that my father had sexually abused me, she told me I was crazy, that nothing like that could have happened. I couldn't believe my ears, because I knew he had molested her, too. He abused her for years before he ever started with me. She even knew that I knew, because I was sometimes in the same room, and she even talked about it with me when I was younger. But when I reminded her of it she denied any such conversation. She just told me that I better be careful and not let him hear me talking like this—that there was no telling what he'd do. I realized then that she was still afraid of him, still under his thumb after all these years."

Yet another reason why you might refuse to believe a sibling's claims of childhood sexual abuse is that to acknowledge the truth would bring back memories of the times when you also abused her.

WHAT IF I AM NOT ABLE TO BELIEVE MY SIBLING?

For any or all of the above reasons, you may not be able at this time to believe your sibling, back her up in the family, or take her side against the perpetrator. Since denial is an *unconscious* defense mechanism, we cannot simply *will* ourselves to remember. You may be unable to recall your sibling's abuse, or your own for that matter for the very same reasons that caused you to block out your memories in the first place: You may still be afraid of the perpetrator and therefore afraid of "telling"; you may not yet be strong enough to face the feelings evoked by the trauma; or you may love the perpetrator so much that you cannot bear to face what he has done.

But even if there are gaps in your memories, sharing with your sibling what you do remember will be of great benefit to her and may even help you regain more of your repressed memories. Together you can piece together your childhood and help each other regain your lost past.

Whether you were abused or not, you both grew up in the same family, and by talking together you can provide each other with valuable help. You have a memory she needs. And she may be able to fill in some gaps in your memory. The functioning of many families is so distorted, so painful, so confusing, that survivors often find it hard to trust their memories. You can confirm for each other that things were as bad as they seemed and that neither of you is crazy.

For a survivor to have even *one* member of her family who is supportive and who validates her reality is invaluable. You are in a position to give a great gift, and the reward for you can be the healing of your own childhood wounds.

Your sibling may become angry with you and even threaten to stop seeing you if you don't believe her or if you are unwilling or unable to speak up and take her side in the family. This is because she feels so betrayed and abandoned by you. But if you can be honest and admit your fears ("I'm sorry, I believe you, but I'm too afraid of Daddy to take your side in front of him"; or "I don't want to hurt Mama"), your sibling may understand. By showing support for her in the following ways, you can let her know that you care, even if you can't do everything she needs right now:

- Listen to her tell her story. This will help you work past your own denial
- Share what you do remember about your childhood
- Read books on childhood sexual abuse so you can understand your sibling better
- Agree to go to therapy together.

Do what you can to support your sibling, but do not allow her to take out on you all the anger that she may be afraid to release at the perpetrator or your parents. In other words, do not take the blame for the following list of possible grievances:

1. NOT PROTECTING HER WHEN SHE WAS A CHILD.

You were a child, too, and a victim of the same dysfunctional family. Often older siblings feel they are somehow responsible for their younger siblings, especially if their parents have forced this responsibility on them. But no matter how much older than your sibling you were, no matter how often you were put in charge of her you are not her parent and therefore are not responsible for what happened to her.

My client Sara shared with me the reason she blamed her sister for not stopping her brother from abusing her:

"I couldn't tell my mother about my brother molesting me, but I was finally able to tell my sister, Marsha. I loved her so much and thought of her as a mother, so I thought she would do something to stop him. But she did nothing. She told me not to worry about it, that things like that happen, that it was no big deal. I was devastated. I couldn't understand why she would talk to me like that, why she seemed so uncaring. It wasn't until recently that I understand. Now I know beyond a shadow of a doubt that she was abused by him, too. She didn't do anything for me because she felt so helpless to stop him from abusing her. She probably did think it was just the way life is."

2. NOT TELLING SOMEONE.

You were probably afraid that if you told you would get in trouble or not be believed. The perpetrator may have intimidated you so much, or have been so abusive to you (either verbally, emotionally, physically, or sexually) that you were petrified of him. Or you may have been afraid of disrupting the family.

3. FEELING JEALOUS OF THE ATTENTION THAT SHE WAS GETTING FROM THE PERPETRATOR.

You were too young to understand that the special attention your sibling received from the perpetrator was his way of manipulating her into doing his bidding or paying her off in order to keep her quiet. It is perfectly natural for you to have felt jealous of what you thought was preferential treatment for no apparent reason.

4. TAKING THE PERPETRATOR'S SIDE.

Perpetrators sometimes deliberately set one sibling against another. In this way, they can be assured that other family members will not get together and gang up on them. For example, an abusive father may encourage his son to dislike and disrespect his sister by making disparaging remarks about females in general or about his daughter in particular.

No one but the perpetrator is responsible for the sexual abuse. You were a victim, too. While you were not to blame for any of the above actions, you may still want to apologize to your sibling for not being able to give her the support she needed as a child. This apology will do wonders for you, for your sibling, and for your relationship. You have been carrying around a tremendous amount of guilt, and while you really weren't responsible for her, this apology will help to relieve that guilt. An apology from you will have a profound effect on your sibling. It will make her feel like you understand her pain, her feelings of betrayal, and her need for support. And it may heal the wedge between you and her that was caused by the sexual abuse.

It is what you do now to show support for your sibling that counts, not what you did or didn't do as a child. As Tina explained to me:

"I didn't feel that my brother Robert protected me as a child, and for a long time I was angry with him about that. I thought he should have stopped my oldest brother, Charles, even if he had to fight him to do it. But all that anger went away when I told him about Charles abusing me. I wasn't sure Robert would admit he knew, but he did. He told me he was behind me all the way and that he was sorry he couldn't protect me when I was a kid. He had been just as terrified of him as I was! But he really came through for me. He went with me the day I confronted Charles. And when Charles started to deny it, Robert backed me up completely, telling my brother that he remembered it, too. I knew that Robert was as afraid of Charles as I was, and that made me love him even more for being willing to support me."

If You Also Sexually Abused Your Sibling

You may have been the person I wrote about earlier, the sibling who, having been sexually abused yourself, turned to someone smaller and less powerful than you to vent your anger on. Unable to express your anger toward the perpetrator, you may have vented your anger on one or more of your siblings. Or, in an attempt to protect yourself from the humiliation of the abuse or to feel as powerful as your oppressor, you may have selected as your target those who were more helpless and dependent than yourself. Since you hated yourself for being weak and helpless, you hated others who were weak as well. This behavior may have begun in childhood and continued into adulthood.

As a child who was introduced to sex too early, you may have initiated sex play with other children in an attempt to deal with the reality you experienced. As Kim remembered, "I'd have friends over, and we'd be playing dolls, and I'd start to make the dolls do sexual things with each other. My friends would say, 'This isn't any fun' and would want to stop, but I was really into it. I felt almost compelled to do it. I think I even felt a little excited about it. It feels awful now to think of it."

This play started right after she was first molested by her father.

It is common for victims, because they were already sexualized, to have sexual feelings toward other children. They may initiate sexual play and even sexual intercourse with children younger than themselves as a way of feeling powerful or as a way of acting out their pain and anger. Many victims fondled their siblings' genitals or the genitals of other children.

Fran confessed to me during one of our sessions, "I remember feeling appalled at myself one time when I was baby-sitting for my little brother. While I was changing his diapers, I was suddenly overwhelmed with the desire to touch his penis. I felt sexually excited and also angry. I wanted to hurt him like I had been hurt. I felt so afraid and disgusted with myself, but I just couldn't seem to stop myself."

At this point, Fran broke down and began to sob. Even though her sobbing continued for well over 20 minutes, I knew she needed to cry the tears she had held in for so many years. Afterward, Fran was able to talk with me about the enormous guilt she had been carrying around.

After several more sessions, Fran came to understand that while she had in fact sexually molested her younger brother, she had done so because she herself had been sexually abused and was reenacting that abuse with her younger brother. While he may have been too young to remember her touching his penis, she still felt compelled to tell him about the incident and to apologize to him. I encouraged her to do this so that she could finally let go of her guilt and because the incident might help her brother to understand feelings that resulted from the experience. Although Fran did not remember doing this again, we had no guarantee that she had not in fact continued the behavior.

Just as Fran did, you need to discover the reasons for your abusive behavior and to work on forgiving yourself for reacting the way you did.

In addition, you owe it to your sibling to tell her about the abuse. She has probably experienced some aftereffects and deserves to have this information so she can seek help.

As it turned out, Fran's brother did not remember the incident or any similar ones. But he did say that he remembered being sexually aroused all the time when he was a child, starting as early as two years old. While it is normal for two-year-old males to play with their penis and even to derive some pleasure from it, her brother said that he started masturbating as early as two, which is unusual. While it is possible that he too was sexually abused by someone else, Fran may have in fact been the one to introduce him to sex and to cause him to be sexualized too early.

At first Fran's brother seemed embarrassed by the whole thing and said he didn't want to talk about it anymore. But several months later, he told Fran that he was glad she had told him, because he had always felt like a "pervert," since none of the other children he was around were as sexual as he was. He had always secretly thought that something was wrong with him. He told her that now he felt better about himself knowing that it wasn't his fault.

Telling your sibling about the molestation will help her to understand herself better. Furthermore, she will feel supported by you as she deals with the rest of your family.

If after telling your sibling about the molestation you still feel horribly guilty or ashamed, you may want to seek professional help. In addition, since there is a strong possibility that you, too, were sexually abused as a child, you will need help to recover from your own wounds.

6

How perpetrators cope when the survivor breaks the silence

You, the person most responsible for the damage not only to the victim but to the rest of your family, will elicit the least sympathy from most professionals. This is not because health-care professionals do not realize the likelihood that you were a victim yourself but because so few perpetrators of childhood sexual abuse are willing to admit their crime and get the help they so desperately need. As a psychotherapist who has worked with both victims and the perpetrators, I do have sympathy for you. I know that you would not have sexually abused a child, least of all a family member, if you were not out of control and if you were not reenacting your own childhood abuse. I know that your life has been plagued by overwhelming feelings of guilt and shame and that no matter how much you have tried to rationalize or excuse what you did, somewhere inside you know that you were wrong.

Unfortunately, I also know from working with perpetrators that no matter how guilty they may feel on the inside, on the outside they are masters at hiding their true feelings and at convincing others that they are innocent. For this reason, most perpetrators do not get the professional assistance that would help them work past their own trauma of childhood abuse and break their compulsion to molest.

Since you are reading this book I will assume that perhaps you are one of the minority, one of the few perpetrators who are willing to face his problems head-on. Perhaps your love for the victim is so great that you are willing to face whatever you have to face in order to help her. Or perhaps the love you have for your spouse, who is threatening to leave you unless you come clean, is motivating you to be more honest with yourself and others.

Even though I will assume that you honestly want to face up to the situation, I can't assume that you will do this easily or willingly. All along the way your tendency to protect yourself by denying the truth will plague you. For this reason I will at times be extremely straightforward as I address you. It may seem that I am being unnecessarily harsh or blunt, but try to remember that my purpose is to encourage you to be brutally honest with yourself in order to push away your tendency to slip back into denial.

THE DISCLOSURE

If someone in your family comes to you and says that she remembers you sexually abused her when she was a child, your first reaction will be shock. Perhaps you will be surprised that she remembers what you did, either because she was very young whenever you molested her or because you gave her drugs or alcohol just prior to each molestation. Or perhaps you are shocked because you have been able to put it out of your own mind for so long that you have almost forgotten it. In any case, your world will suddenly be turned upside down as you are forced to admit that something you did caused someone you care about a great deal of damage.

Although you may feel a tremendous amount of shame and guilt about what you did, and these feelings may have distressed you for a long time, your first instinct may be to defend yourself by denying that the abuse ever happened. You may assume that since no one can prove it actually happened, your best defense is denial. This need to defend yourself may be so strong that it wins out over your sense of right and wrong and even over your love for the victim. Even if there is a part of you that would like to admit it and get it over with once and for all, your need to protect yourself may cause you to lie.

Understand that your tendency to lie and deny what you did is completely natural. Starting when we were small children, we learned to lie to avoid getting into trouble. Since the ramifications of admitting sexual abuse are so extreme, it makes sense that you would not willingly admit to something that could jeopardize your relationships with other family members, your marriage, your career, your standing in the community, or your financial status.

You may tell yourself that it is in the past and that there is nothing you can do about it now. What is done is done. You may rationalize that since you cannot rewrite the past, no good can come from admitting what happened and hurting other people now. After all, you may think, I already hurt my child (or my grandchild, sibling, niece, or nephew), why should I now hurt the rest of my family by admitting it?

The problem with this kind of rationalizing is that it is just that—a way of excusing your behavior. It is a way of shielding yourself and avoiding responsibility and owning up to your mistake. You may try to fool yourself into thinking that you are lying to protect other people, but the truth is you are lying to protect yourself. It is important that you at least try to be honest with yourself.

You may believe that by keeping silent you are doing what is best for the rest of your family, but there is no way for you to know that. You are not God and should not try to play God. You are not in a position to know what is best for your family, because you are not seeing things clearly. Your vision and your judgment are flawed by your need to protect yourself.

You cannot predict what will come of your telling the truth. You may indeed alienate some people from you, but on the other hand you have an equal chance of drawing people closer to you, once you are courageous enough to admit the truth. I can tell you from my many years of working with survivors and their families that those few perpetrators who were brave enough and loving enough to admit the truth were respected far more than those who continued to lie.

The person that you victimized knows what you did, and no amount of denial on your part will change that. By continuing to lie about it, you only lower yourself in her eyes. In fact, the only way you can redeem yourself to this person is to tell the truth. At the very least, she will respect you for being honest. At the most she will love you for loving her enough to tell the truth.

But the survivor is not the only person who knows the truth. Other members of your family also know, or have suspected for a long time. Your denial may temporarily confuse them, and they may even rally to your side and become angry at the survivor for making what they consider to be a false allegation. But secretly, silently, they will wonder, they will question, they will suspect.

WHY SHOULD I ADMIT IT?

The most important reason for you to admit that you sexually abused her is that it will be the most important gift you can ever give your victim. While it is true that you cannot erase the damage you have already caused, you have a chance to lessen that damage by admitting the truth. Your admission will not only validate the perceptions of the survivor, but also be the first step toward healing your relationship. If you love or care about this person, the only way you can show that love is to admit the truth. The only way you can mend the relationship is by telling the truth.

Even though the survivor knows what happened, she needs you to admit it in order to validate her feelings, to justify her reactions, to finally put her mind at ease.

Victims of child sexual abuse feel a tremendous amount of guilt. They feel guilty for the abuse itself, for the things they did as a child as a result of the abuse, and for the things they have done as an adult to hurt themselves and others. To a large extent, a survivor's recovery depends on freeing themselves from this guilt.

Sometimes sexual-abuse victims try to avoid feeling their *helplessness* and *powerlessness* by blaming themselves for the abuse. As a child, as a victim, they were powerless to change the situation, but it may have been too frightening to feel this powerlessness. They may have preferred instead to feel guilty, since at least then they had the *illusion of control* over what was happening to them.

Other victims feel so guilty, ugly, and dirty inside from the sexual abuse that they believe they were and are being punished by God for being "bad." Otherwise, why would such a horrible thing happen to them? They believe that terrible things happen because they deserve it. This belief adds to their guilt.

Many survivors also punish their bodies by mutilating themselves with razors, knives, and pins, starving themselves, or stuffing themselves with food to the point of pain. Some assault their bodies with poison in the form of cigarettes, alcohol, and drugs. The survivor in your life needs your help in order to stop hating her body when it is a perfectly good and normal body. She needs your help in order to understand that her body did not abuse her or betray her—to understand that it was tricked, just like she was by you.

Even though the survivor knows that the sexual abuse wasn't her fault from an intellectual, logical standpoint, she may not have forgiven herself for her involvement in the abuse (being submissive or passive, not telling anyone, having her body respond). This is where you come in. By taking total responsibility for the incident or incidents, you can relieve the survivor of her guilt as well as your own.

But there is another important reason why you need to admit the truth. You need to tell the truth for you. You have been walking around for years carrying this burden, knowing that you were guilty of a horrendous act. Even though you may have successfully justified your actions at times, you have known deep down in your heart that you were guilty of something that is a sin in everyone's eyes. Only by admitting your transgression will you be set free from your burden of guilt and self-loathing; only by acknowledging your guilt will you be forgiven; only by admitting that you have a problem will you be able to get help.

You may not be aware of your guilt. It can be working on you without your knowing it. Just as it is with your victim, unconscious guilt can cause you to be self-destructive by abusing your body with food, alcohol, drugs, cigarettes, or self-mutilation; by being accident-prone; by sabotaging your success; or by eliciting punishment from others.

This unconscious guilt may cause you to keep a tenacious hold on your problems and your pain, because it gives you the punishment you feel you deserve. You may have spent your life punishing yourself with one bad marriage after another, one illness after another.

Admitting the sexual abuse will go a long way toward relieving you of this burden of guilt. Instead of continuing to live in fear that you will be found out, instead of punishing yourself or your body for your sins, take this opportunity to come clean. Try to balance out the harm you have done by doing something that will help the survivor and your family. Expose the secrets and give your family a chance at a new, healthier life. Do it for them and for you.

BUT WHAT IF I REALLY DIDN'T DO IT?

I have never had a client who claimed to be abused when she wasn't. Early on in therapy some clients are confused about just who their perpetrator was. For example, they may vacillate between thinking that it was their father or their grandfather. But eventually, most clients do become clear about who their abuser was. I have never known a client to confront someone without knowing that he was indeed the perpetrator.

So why would someone say you sexually abused her as a child if it wasn't true? What possible reason could she have to say such a thing? If you honestly don't remember what your loved one is telling you, then it is possible (but not probable) that you may have forgotten the event or events—that you may have *blocked it out of your memory.* If you were so traumatized by the act of abusing someone you loved that you could not tolerate having a memory of it, it is *possible* that you may have protected yourself from this memory by repressing it. There have also been some rare cases when the perpetrator was in an alcoholic blackout, or sleepwalking, and thus has no memory of the abuse.

I want to warn you, though, that these lapses are rare and only occur in very specific situations. Using the excuse that you don't have any memory of the abuse could get you into more trouble than it's worth, because professionals can spot a liar a mile away. If you really do remember but you're thinking of using these rare situations as an easy way out, think again.

If you in fact do not remember sexually abusing your loved one, stating that you have no memory of it still does not get you off the hook. Not remembering does not mean you are exempt from taking responsibility for your actions.

Let's say you were involved in a hit-and-run accident in which you hit a pedestrian and then fled from the scene. Traumatized by the incident, you repressed the memory of it to the point that in your mind the event never took place. When, several weeks later, the police come to your door and arrest you, you are completely taken by surprise. Insisting on your innocence, you are certain there has been some kind of mistake. But the police have eye witnesses who took down your license-plate number and the make and model of your car. Now you are certain that someone else must have been driving your car, and you search your memory for a time when you loaned it to someone else. When no such memory comes, you scramble for another explanation: maybe someone used your car without permission. "Yes, that must be it—someone else used my car without my knowing it," you tell yourself and the police. But the police aren't having any of it. People just don't go around "borrowing" other people's cars, getting into hit-and-run accidents, and then returning the car to the owner—all without the owner's knowing about it. And there is another troubling bit of evidence. It seems that you took your car to a garage the day after the accident and had repair work done on your grille and had a headlight replaced. Not only did the garage mechanic identify you, but the police have a copy of the work order with your signature on it. Now you are completely overwhelmed. There seems to be no other way around it—you were the driver of the car that severely injured another human being. It seems that before you repressed the memory of the accident you managed to attempt to cover your tracks by getting the car fixed. Memory or no, don't you think you should be held responsible for the accident and for fleeing the scene? Certainly the police, the courts, the family of the victim, and the victim herself hold you responsible.

Now let's compare this analogy with the issue at hand. Even though you say you have no memory of the abuse, you will have to take responsibility for your actions. You can try to argue that it was someone else who did the crime, or that someone or something else had control over your body, but it was in fact you who abused that child. Although you can argue that in this case there is none of the kind of evidence there was in the hit-and-run, the eyewitness testimony of your victim is evidence enough.

The point here is that even if you have repressed the memory of abusing a child, the fact that she is coming forward now and saying that you abused her is all the proof you need. Since there is absolutely no reason for her to lie, you will have to take her word for it, at least in terms of realizing that you need psychotherapy in order to uncover your memories. Refusing to do this is tantamount to not taking responsibility for your actions.

COULD I HAVE BEEN DRUNK AND BLOCKED IT OUT?

For those of you who believe that you may have been in an alcoholic blackout and are therefore not responsible for your actions, let's use our analogy of the hit-and-run accident again, but this time let's say you were drunk and in a blackout when you hit the woman. Does this make you any less responsible for hitting her? Does this mean that the next morning, when you awoke from your alcoholic stupor with no memory of the accident, you were immune to the consequences of your actions?

We know that alcohol does lower our inhibitions and that we sometimes do things while drunk that we wouldn't ordinarily do. But most of the perpetrators I have worked with who were drunk at the time they molested a child acknowledge that they had had thoughts of having sex with the child long before they actually did it. They remember being sexually aroused by the child and having sexual fantasies involving her even when they were sober. And while the alcohol may have acted as a disinhibitor, giving them permission to do something they might not have done while sober, the alcohol did not *cause* or *create* their problem.

As a matter of fact, most of the perpetrators I have worked with who abuse alcohol have come to realize that alcohol abuse was a *symptom* of a far deeper problem—most often, the sexual abuse that they themselves suffered as a child. Because they felt so damaged, guilty, ashamed, and worthless, they sought solace in alcohol to help them out of their depressions. And because they felt so inadequate and fearful of social and sexual relationships, they used alcohol to give them the courage to connect with other people and to feel socially acceptable.

TAKING RESPONSIBILITY

Even if you are willing to admit that you sexually abused your relative, you may not be willing to take complete responsibility for your actions. Next to denying the childhood sexual abuse entirely, the most common thing that perpetrators do is to make excuses for their behavior. Blaming either the child, their spouse, or someone else is a common excuse. Often, even those who do admit being the seducer do not accept responsibility for the incidents. The following are some of the most common excuses made by perpetrators for their actions.

But I am not related to this person. It is acceptable for an adult to have sex with a child as long as the child is not a relative.

It is no more acceptable for an adult to have sex with an unrelated child than it is for him to have sex with his own offspring. In fact, many victims of sexual abuse view their perpetrator as they would view a relative: They looked up to him and trusted him and they feel betrayed. This is so often the case that the definition of *incest* has been broadened to include any sexual contact between a child and someone *the child views as a relative.*

It is the *betrayal of trust* that is so damaging for a child who is sexually abused, because children, in their vulnerability, depend upon and look up to adults to take care of them, not to exploit them and use them for their own needs.

While childhood sexual abuse is much more widespread than we once realized, it is nonetheless utterly wrong. A child's immature intellectual and emotional structure is not equipped for a sexual awakening, and sexual abuse can damage him or her for life.

But I was teaching her about sex so she would grow up to be a good lover.

You are not being honest with yourself if you tell yourself this. Children don't need hands-on experience with an adult in order to learn how to be good lovers. First of all, children need their developmental years in which to play and grow freely, unencumbered by sex. They need their time of innocence to mature and develop emotionally and sexually at their own speed, not to be introduced to it before they are ready. Then, as young adults ready to learn about sex, they can embark on the adventure with age-appropriate sex partners of their own choice.

In addition, victims whose parents (usually their fathers) told them they were teaching them about sex tend to suffer from many sexual problems as adults. They report feeling stigmatized and confused about sexual and nonsexual encounters, engaging in compulsive sexual activities, or wanting to avoid all sexual activity.

Saying that you were "teaching" your child is a worn-out rationalization. Though many perpetrators use it, it has absolutely no grounds in research or reality.

I suffer from a mental disorder, or I was "temporarily insane" when I committed this crime.

Some professionals do consider child molesters to be emotionally disturbed, but at no time are they rendered incapable of assuming responsibility for their actions.

In psychotherapeutic jargon, many child molesters suffer from a disorder called pedophilia, a specific combination of "deviant arousal" and "character disorder." In lay terms, this means the molester is both sexually excited by children and sees nothing wrong with gratifying himself at their expense. Although there is a consensus among the experts that pedophiles do not consciously choose to be attracted to children, they do choose to act on their urges. No matter how much he may himself have been deprived or victimized, the child molester is still responsible for his actions. People who are sexually attracted to children do not have to act on this attraction. There are several options: to make certain never to be left alone with a child; to seek professional help; to warn other family members of the attraction.

Some argue that the child molester is out of control, that he has a compulsion to sexually abuse children, just as some people have a compulsion to drink or overeat. Child molesters are out of control and they do need help. But we must not fall into the trap of excusing their behavior on these grounds. Over and over in talking with perpetrators, therapists have observed that they did know right from wrong, they did know they needed help, but they chose not to get it. They are generally more bent on denying responsibility for their actions and finding ways of continuing their behavior than they are on seeking help.

Child molesters generally fall into one of two categories: the sociopath and the self-deceiver. The sociopath has no moral qualms about hurting others to get what he wants. He simply doesn't have any regard for others' feelings. He seems to have his own set of values that do not correspond to society's values. This character disorder is manifested by a lack of empathy for the victim, little regard for social taboos, and poor impulse control.

The self-deceiver, on the other hand, minimizes the harm he causes and projects the blame onto the victim or his wife. He employs defense mechanisms to keep a grip on his sanity. The use of defense mechanisms is quite normal, but offenders use them in excessive ways.

The child chose to have sex with me.

The survivor cannot be held responsible for any so-called "choices" she made concerning the sexual abuse, because she was incapable of making a *free* choice. A free choice is made when you understand the consequences of your actions and when you are not coerced, bribed, intimidated, or threatened into satisfying the perverse desires of someone else.

In his book *Child Sexual Abuse*, David Finkelhor discusses the ethical dimension of consent. He noted that even though children sometimes appear to consent passively or even to cooperate, they are actually incapable of truly consenting to sex with adults because of the fact that they *are* children. He further stated that for consent truly to occur, two conditions must exist: a person must know what it is that he or she is consenting to, and must have true freedom to say yes or no. A child does not have the freedom to say yes or no. Children lack the necessary information to make an informed decision, since they are ignorant about sex—the mechanics of it as well as the social meanings of sexuality. Finkelhor states: "For example, they are unlikely to be aware of the rules and regulations surrounding sexual intimacy—what it is supposed to signify. They are uninformed and inexperienced about what criteria to use in judging the acceptability of a sexual partner. They do not know much about the 'natural history' of a sexual relationship, what course it will take. And finally, children have little way of knowing how other people are likely to react to the experience they are about to undertake—what likely consequences it will have for them in the future."

The survivor is blameless for her sexual involvement with you. She was just a child, incapable of making such a decision, emotionally unequipped to handle such a grown-up matter. Even if she was a teenager when the abuse occurred, he or she was still too young to be having sex with an adult.

The child enjoyed it.

Our bodies may respond to touch, no matter who is doing the touching. Your victim's body may have responded to the touching, no matter how much her *mind* fought it or felt repulsed by it. Some victims have experienced orgasm even though they were being traumatized, hated the perpetrator, or were terrified. This betrayal by their body is sometimes the hardest to forgive. A child does not know that her body can respond without her consent, or even that it can respond in such a way at all. She and you may conclude that she must have wanted the sexual act, that she must have asked for it in some way, otherwise, why would her body feel pleasure? In addition, you may have used the fact that her body was responding to manipulate her into believing that she really wanted it.

I was a victim of childhood sexual abuse myself, and I was just repeating the cycle of abuse by molesting another child.

It is true that the majority of perpetrators were sexually abused as children. It has been estimated that between 60 and 100 percent of all sex offenders have experienced some form of early sexual victimization. Such victimization is believed to underlie the attraction to and victimization of children. But victimizing helpless children does not *undo* the childhood trauma that the perpetrator experienced. There is no excuse for continuing the cycle of abuse, and not all victims of childhood sexual abuse necessarily repeat the pattern. Consider, for example, that women seldom molest children, even though more girls are molested than boys. Many victims in fact seek help in order *not* to continue the cycle.

As a victim of childhood sexual abuse yourself, you know the damage that is caused by such an action. You know the pain, fear, anger, guilt, shame, and sense of betrayal that you felt because of the abuse. And you know how important it is for the perpetrator to acknowledge his responsibility for his actions and not to blame the child.

If you blame yourself for the abuse that you suffered, or if you are unable to feel angry toward your own abuser, you are in denial about your own victimization. This denial may have contributed to your continuing the cycle of abuse. Once you admit what you did and seek the professional help you so desperately need, you will become more clear about your own and your victim's innocence.

I *was not getting my sexual and emotional needs met by my spouse.*

Perpetrators rarely sexually abuse children to satisfy purely sexual needs. Instead, they do it in order to meet a number of emotional needs: to exercise power over someone; to seek revenge against a wife or mother for neglectful or abusive treatment; or to seek from the child that which they lack so desperately in themselves (love, innocence, approval). Many child molesters are in fact unable to maintain a sexual relationship with an adult woman because of overriding feelings of inadequacy and insecurity.

Other perpetrators are sex addicts who use sex as a distraction from their problems, as a way of stuffing their emotions, or as a way of temporarily building up their low self-esteem. Some perpetrators have been known to have sex with their wives two, three, or even four times a day in addition to molesting children.

You didn't sexually abuse your own child or someone else's because your spouse wasn't paying enough attention to you or wasn't giving you enough sex. You did it because of problems that you had before you ever got married, problems that began in your childhood. If you reached out to a child for affection and attention it was because you have been feeling deprived and neglected for a long, long time, not just in your marriage.

IS THERE ANY HOPE? FOR ME? FOR MY FAMILY?

There is hope for change, but first you must openly admit your actions and take full responsibility for the abuse. You must admit the gravity of your offense and let down your armor of rationalization. Then you must work on your problems every day for the rest of your life, much like a recovering alcoholic. Many authorities believe that although sex offenders can never be "cured," they can learn to control their sexually deviant behavior.

The hope for you lies in your seeking professional help, so that you can come to understand why it was that you sexually abused a child (or children). Whether it was because you yourself were sexually abused, extremely neglected or deprived of love, brutally beaten, or emotionally abused as a child, the reason for your behavior must be uncovered and understood.

My own clinical experience has taught me that the only time a child molester seems to have any hope of recovery is when he not only admits to himself that he has a problem but also admits it to others. It is especially important to admit to your family and to the victim that you are entirely responsible for the abuse. Even though it is extremely rare for a child molester to recognize and assume full responsibility for the pain and suffering he has inflicted, if you are sincere in your admission of guilt, if you ask the victim for forgiveness and offer real assurance that she was not responsible in any way, and if you commit yourself to change through therapy or self-help groups such as Parents United, there is some hope for real change.

It is vitally important that you believe the survivor when she discloses the abuse to you. Even if some of her assertions sound improbable to you, there is truth to everything she is saying. While parts of her story may be missing, while she may not yet be able to clearly identify who the perpetrator was or what the circumstances were, believe her when she tells you she was abused. She will be able to fill in the details as she progresses in her recovery.

When the survivor was being sexually abused, those around her (including you) acted as if it wasn't happening. Since no one acknowledged the abuse, she sometimes felt that it wasn't real. Because the abuser didn't acknowledge her pain, she may have thought that perhaps it wasn't as bad as she felt it was.

Coming out of denial and telling the truth about what happened to them as children is an important step for survivors of childhood sexual abuse. Unless they face the truth, they cannot fully recover. This means telling those close to them exactly what happened without minimizing it or denying their feelings about it. By doing this, they confirm for themselves that they didn't imagine it.

Questioning the accuracy of the survivor's disclosure can reinforce the idea that her perceptions are inaccurate, flawed, or distorted and will encourage her to go back into denial. In the rare situation where the survivor can hold onto the truth in the face of disbelief, the doubt of another family member can nonetheless damage and even destroy whatever trust there was between them.

If you don't believe what the survivor is telling you yet, continue working on it until you do. Let her know that your reaction to the news was powerful and that even though you still do not want to believe the sexual abuse occurred, you are open to the possibility. If you want to believe her but just can't, tell her so and add that you are working on it by learning all you can about childhood sexual abuse.

Once you have acknowledged the reality of the sexual abuse and the truth about your family situation when it occurred, you, the survivor, and the rest of your family are well on your way toward recovery. It is important to continue an open dialogue with the survivor. If you do not bring up the issue again, she may think you want to sweep it under the carpet. Periodically, ask her how she is doing, how her therapy is going, how she feels about herself and you. Make certain that when you ask, you are truly willing to hear and acknowledge the answer. When the abuse took place, the survivor was forced to suffer alone. Just knowing that you are concerned and that you care about her can ease the pain and accelerate healing. And, if you are a parent, know that although your child may receive support from others (her mate, her friends, her therapist or support group), when a parent gives supportive caring the effect is powerfully healing.

PART II

HOW TO SUPPORT EACH OTHER THROUGHOUT RECOVERY

Since childhood sexual abuse causes so much damage in a family, it will take the entire family working together to achieve maximum healing, either for the individuals or for the family unit. Each family member should spend some time thinking about the others' feelings and needs. Having empathy for one another will go a long way toward healing wounds, renewing trust, and resolving conflicts.

Supporting each other throughout the healing process involves many things. It means being patient with one another as each of you struggles with your own difficulties, understanding that coming to terms with childhood sexual abuse is painful and takes time. It means trying not to judge one another too quickly or too harshly when denial sets in; encouraging one another to seek outside help whenever necessary; and not interfering with each other's therapy or recovery programs. The following two chapters, one for survivors and one for other family members, will outline ways in which you can support your loved ones.

7

HOW TO SUPPORT OTHER FAMILY MEMBERS

For Survivors

It stands to reason that as the survivor of abuse, you will need support from your family throughout your recovery. What's perhaps less obvious is that your family will also need support from you. While it is important that you allow yourself to express whatever emotions you feel toward them, completely closing your heart and mind will curtail any possibility of the family's working this problem out together. Your assistance to other family members will mainly consist of working on your attitudes toward them. The following are some suggestions as to how to go about this.

Remember that childhood sexual abuse is a family problem.

Although you were the obvious victim, each person in your family was also damaged to some extent by the abuse, and each needs help in order to heal from this damage. Your nonoffending parent will need help coping with the news that you were abused and that someone in your family or someone your family trusted did the abusing. The perpetrator betrayed not only your trust but that of your parent(s) as well.

There's a strong likelihood that your siblings were sexually abused by the same perpetrator. Even if they weren't, they suffer from the guilt they feel—because they were glad it was you who was being abused and not they, because they didn't protect you, or because they didn't tell.

In addition, remember that childhood sexual abuse is passed down from one generation to the next. While you have a right to be angry with your mother, for example, for not protecting you, the chances are very high that she, too, was sexually abused as a child, especially if the perpetrator in your case was your father, your stepfather, or your mother's boyfriend. While males tend to continue the cycle of abuse by victimizing others, females who were sexually abused as children tend to repeat the pattern of abuse by marrying or getting involved with child molesters.

Even though your mother may have put you in danger because of her involvement with a perpetrator, she was probably acting out what is called a *repetition compulsion*, an unconscious attempt to rewrite the past—to master and change past events by getting involved with someone like her abuser. While you still have a right to be angry with her, try to remember that she was a victim, too, and that she probably never meant to hurt you.

If the perpetrator was your parent's father, uncle, or sibling, you can be quite sure that your parent was molested by the very same person. Because she repressed the memory of the abuse or in some other way was in denial about it, she was unable to recognize the danger when the same abuser began to molest you.

Parents who are in denial about their own childhood sexual abuse are not able to protect their children from the same or other abusers. They have such an investment in protecting themselves from their own memories that they simply *do not see* the abuse or its telltale symptoms in their own children. Even parents who do remember their own abuse are likely to deny that the same thing is happening to their child unless they have received therapy, because they are afraid to face their feelings about it.

Realize that each family member has reasons for his behavior.

Your mother ignored or was blind to signs of abuse because she cannot face the pain of her own abuse. Your sibling grew up in the same dysfunctional, abusive, or alcoholic family that you did and therefore is also a victim of emotional, physical, or sexual abuse. And your father, mother, sibling, uncle, or grandparent—whoever was the perpetrator—was sexually, physically, or emotionally abused as a child. This fact does not excuse their behavior, but it does explain their actions and may make them more human in your eyes.

Remember that childhood sexual abuse is a very difficult thing to face.

Remind yourself of how long it has taken you to come out of denial, how painful facing the truth was, and how much you resisted it. It has taken you months and in some cases years to fully acknowledge what happened to you and how much the abuse damaged you. It may have taken the assistance of a therapist or a support group to help you face your repressed feelings toward the perpetrator and other family members. Remind yourself of how you initially protected or made excuses for your perpetrator and other family members, how you minimized the damage, how you blamed yourself instead of allowing yourself to feel your anger.

Your family will need to go through the same time-consuming, painful process before they can admit exactly what happened, as Roseanne experienced:

"When my mother didn't believe me, I felt devastated. I felt as if I'd lost not only my father but now my mother as well. I felt like an orphan. Then my therapist encouraged me to give my mother some time to think about the whole situation and to give her some books to read on the subject, instead of giving up on her.

"I did this, and then I started asking her to lunch, just the two of us. I wanted to talk about the sexual abuse, but it was clear she didn't, so I left it alone for a while. I just told her that I really needed her support and that if she had any questions, I'd be happy to answer them. When it felt too painful to be around her—like the time she was insensitive enough to tell me all about what a wonderful time she had on a vacation with my father—I would tell her I'd have to stay away for a while in order to take care of myself. Each time I did this she'd call me up later on and apologize for being insensitive, and we'd try again. This all seemed to take forever, but over time my mother and I slowly began to know one another and establish the kind of bond a mother and daughter are supposed to have."

"Eventually, my mother was able to tell me that she had always felt like I was more of a threat than a daughter—that she was always jealous of the attention my father paid me. As we talked about this, it all began to make sense to her, and she actually began to believe me. Suddenly, I wasn't the person who was stealing her husband away from her, but her daughter who needed her protection and support. I am so glad now that I didn't write her off right away when she didn't believe me, that I hung in there with her until she could face the truth."

Remember that it takes time to change and that significant change is always very difficult.

At times it will seem to you that your family will never change. They may seem to understand how you feel one day, only to regress and ignore or minimize your feelings the next. They may tell you they believe you, only to change their minds later on. Your parent(s) may apologize for not protecting you better, only to turn around and deny that the abuse ever happened, discount the damage, or blame you for your own abuse.

Any kind of significant change is extremely difficult to accomplish, but the kinds of changes your family is going to need to make are monumental. Your parent(s) will have to face the painful fact that they did not protect you well enough, and the entire family will have to change their perceptions of themselves and of each other. In addition, you and they will need to learn different ways of communicating so that there is a lot more listening and a lot less blaming. Instead of demanding the needed changes right away, be grateful if family members show any sign of willingness to change .

In addition to the attitudinal changes listed above, there are some specific things you will need to do for other family members in order to support them and facilitate healing. Keep in mind that your main focus should be on your own recovery, and never sacrifice your own well-being or recovery for your family.

Do not pressure your parents or other members of your family into believing you, admitting they were wrong, or seeking help.

Members of your family will not react well to pressure from you. In fact, trying to force them will probably have the opposite effect.

Realize that family members have their reasons for wanting not to believe you. Perhaps they do not want to have to sever their relationship with the perpetrator, or to face their own abuse, or to face the pain involved. Whatever the reason, each person must come to terms with the abuse in his own time.

Understand that most parents, even those who seem to deny responsibility, secretly hold themselves responsible for the safety and welfare of their child. Although your parents may have become defensive when you told them about the abuse, or even blamed you for allowing it to happen, underneath it all they probably feel they have only themselves to blame and are afraid of censure from you or from others.

While you can encourage your family to seek professional help, they will only do so if and when they are ready. Even those family members who do go for help will need time to assimilate all the new information and to get past their denial. It usually takes many months of therapy before parents are able to recognize their part in the sexual abuse of their own child.

Try to reach a balance between being patient with your family and excusing their behavior.

It will take a lot of patience on your part to wait for your family to come out of denial, and patience is something you may not have very much of at this point. Furthermore, not all survivors can afford to continue struggling with their family, because they have already done so for far too long. You must ask yourself, "Can I be patient without enabling other family members to continue their abusive, addictive, or otherwise harmful behavior? Can I continue struggling with them without losing myself?"

Survivors have a very difficult time remaining separate from their families. Therefore, they sometimes go to extremes in order to maintain a separate sense of self and to retain their perceptions. In the beginning of their recovery, many survivors actually need to stay away from their parents or other members of their family of origin in order to develop a stronger sense of self and belief in their perceptions.

But as difficult as it may seem, it is possible to come to a place where you can maintain your sense of self *and* work with your family. And with time and work on your part, you can learn to listen to other family members' sides of the story and grow to understand why they acted as they did, without running the risk of losing your anger or your own perceptions, or of excusing or minimizing the role they played in the abuse. It is also possible for you to learn to distinguish between when it is appropriate and healthy to express your righteous anger and when it is not. You can learn to limit the expression of your anger to times when it will be heard, instead of randomly and constantly berating family members in a way that is abusive or ineffectual.

Don't blame other family members for what the perpetrator did.

While your nonoffending parent(s) may not have protected you sufficiently, may have been absent either emotionally or physically, or may not have made it easy for you to tell them about the abuse, they are not, in fact, responsible for what the perpetrator did. It is vitally important that you become very clear about this.

For example, Jennifer was extremely angry with her mother for marrying her stepfather and for leaving her alone with him at night while she worked. She blamed her mother for the fact that she was sexually abused by him because she felt that her mother should have never married such a man and that she shouldn't have trusted him to be alone with her daughter. But Jennifer needed to make a distinction between being angry with her mother for her poor judgment and blaming her for the actual abuse that she experienced.

In order to help yourself make this distinction, make a separate list of all the reasons why you are angry with each family member, including the perpetrator. If you find that you are tending to blame other family members for what the perpetrator did, refer back to your lists as a reminder.

In addition, it is important to realize that many survivors fall into the trap of staying angry with their (nonoffending) parent(s) rather than getting angry with the actual perpetrator. Since many perpetraters were very frightening people who threatened great bodily harm or even death if the survivor ever told, it may feel safer to direct your anger toward your parents. Even if the perpetrator is dead or it would be impossible for him to find you, the threat may be no less real in your mind.

Encourage other family members to seek professional help or to join a 12-step program or Parents United.

Encouraging other family members to seek outside help for themselves is distinctly different from pressuring them to go into therapy. As mentioned earlier, your parents and siblings will also need support in order for them to heal from the devastation of childhood sexual abuse, but you cannot be expected to provide all the support they will need. They, just like you, will need help from outside sources. Recommend that your parents or siblings have a few sessions of individual therapy from someone who specializes in working with the issue of childhood sexual abuse. If they think of it as only a few sessions, they might be more willing to explore the option of counseling than if they're presented with the idea of long-term therapy. Once they experience what counseling is like, they may be willing to continue long-term.

If they resist the idea of counseling or therapy, suggest they join a support group for family members of survivors. Explain to them that such groups will help them feel like they are not alone with their problems and that the groups offer solutions to some of the most difficult aspects of being a relative of a survivor.

ADDITIONAL TIPS ON HOW TO SUPPORT YOUR (NONOFFENDING) PARENTS

Your parents come from another generation in which childhood sexual abuse was never spoken of, much less focused on the way it is today. They didn't hear about sexual abuse on television, nor were they taught to recognize symptoms. They had no idea how prevalent such abuse is. And as I mentioned earlier, even if they were sexually abused themselves, they were probably in denial about it and therefore not looking for symptoms in their own children.

Remember that in your parents' generation, psychotherapy was viewed as something that only really crazy people needed. Your parents may need to have it explained to them that nowadays many people seek the help of professional therapists, not because they are mentally disturbed but because they need someone who is objective and trained to help them understand themselves better and to get through difficult times. Don't be surprised if your parents don't trust therapists or therapy or if they think the whole thing is a big waste of time and money. Sit down with them and try to educate them about how therapy works, sharing your own experience with them and telling them how much it has helped you.

In addition, try to understand how very difficult it will be for your parents to be forced to choose between you and another family member who was your perpetrator. While you may feel that any good parent would choose her own child over her spouse, don't underestimate the pain that goes into such a decision. And if the decision is between you and another one of their children the decision is nearly impossible.

While you are coming from the place of being a victim who has been wronged and you cannot imagine a parent siding with the abuser, your parent will be coming from the perspective of having to choose between two people she loves equally, not between someone who is "good" and someone who is "bad."

ADDITIONAL TIPS ON HOW TO SUPPORT YOUR SIBLINGS

The best way for you to support a sibling is to allow her to face the truth in her own time, without pressuring her or trying to influence her in any way. For example, your sibling may have told you that she remembered that your father also molested her, only to "forget" that she told you or to change her mind and take it all back. Recognize that she may need to go in and out of denial for some time before she can finally admit the truth to herself or to anyone else. Don't try to push her into facing anything she is not prepared to face yet.

It is also important to realize that as children your siblings may have had a perception of your family life and of the perpetrator that was entirely different from yours. Even though they more than likely experienced the same things you did—deprivation, neglect, and emotional, verbal, or physical abuse—they may have played a different role in the family or developed a different way of coping, and therefore may perceive the situation very differently from you. For example, an abusive parent may have become progressively worse, and so older children may not have suffered as much abuse as younger ones. Or the reverse could be true—your parent may have "mellowed with age" or stopped drinking and treated younger children better. Sometimes one or both parents will favor one child over the others, or will dislike and single out one child. Any of these variables can contribute to each sibling's having a different perception of what their childhood was like.

If your sibling sees your perpetrator as a wonderful person, don't expect her to believe you right away when you tell her about the abuse. It will be extremely difficult for her to change her perception of a loving father into one who is capable of sexually abusing his own child. In fact, your sibling will have an emotional investment in *not* believing you.

You cannot change your family. Nor can you force family members into making the necessary changes that are going to be required in order for your family to heal from the devastation of childhood sexual abuse. Each family member will need to find his own way through the maze of fear, denial, anger, and pain—all the feelings they will eventually go through as they struggle first with deciding whether or not they believe that the abuse actually occurred and then with deciding how to proceed from there. All you can do is to try to be as patient as possible without compromising your own recovery and as empathetic about their pain and fears as possible without losing track of your own emotions.

8

HOW TO SUPPORT THE SURVIVOR

For Family Members Other Than the Offending Relative

A s I have mentioned earlier, the survivor in your family desperately needs your support in order to recover from the damage caused by the sexual abuse. This doesn't mean that you put your own feelings aside entirely, just that you remember that as much as you are hurting over this situation, the person who was sexually abused is hurting even more. In addition to coping with the devastating wounds of childhood sexual abuse, she must carry the burden of knowing that she has brought you the news that has put your family in a turmoil, caused you to have to change your perceptions about the perpetrator, and possibly caused you to end your relationship with the perpetrator. These are heavy burdens indeed. As much as possible, try to lighten them by being as supportive of the survivor as possible.

You will also be helping yourself and the rest of your family by following the suggestions I outline in this chapter. As you know, conflicts between the survivor and other family members are a common occurrence. Because most of these conflicts are caused by the survivor's feeling unsupported by other family members, the more supported the survivor feels, the lower the chances of family conflict. This in turn will make life easier for everyone involved.

How to Best Support the Survivor

1. Tell the survivor that you believe her (if you do).
2. Tell her it was not her fault.
3. Work on recognizing what part you had (or didn't have) in allowing the abuse to occur or in causing misunderstanding between you.
4. Apologize to the survivor for whatever you have done to hurt her.
5. Recognize that she has a right to her anger toward you.
6. Stand up for her against the perpetrator.
7. Back her up in the family.
8. Ask the survivor what you can do *now* to support her.
9. Try to be understanding if she can't be around you
10. Get help for yourself.
11. Learn how your family situation contributed to the abuse.
12. Support the survivor throughout the recovery process.
    - Learn all you can about sexual abuse and the healing process.
    - Allow the survivor the time and space to release her anger.
    - Allow the survivor to blame others for a while.
    - Allow the survivor the time and space to feel her pain.
    - Respect the time and space it takes to heal.
    - Understand that you must earn the survivor's trust.
    - Don't try to rescue the survivor.
    - Support the survivor in her changes.

Tell the survivor that you believe her.

Survivors need you to tell them that you believe them for several reasons. First of all, as children enduring such abuse, they assumed no one would believe them if they told. And so they held in the secret, for months, years, and even decades. Because they held in the secret so long, they began to doubt their own perceptions and memories. As they enter therapy or begin a recovery program, they are encouraged to trust their perceptions and trust their recollections of the past. One word of disbelief from someone they care about, however, can throw them right back into self-doubt.

One of the most damaging things that can happen to a survivor is not to be believed. This is because so many survivors were not believed when they tried to tell or when they tried to get help as children. The survivor in your family is not lying or exaggerating. If anything, survivors of childhood sexual abuse tend to minimize what happened, how much it hurt them, and how terrible they feel about it.

Although the things a survivor tells you may seem totally unbelievable to you—either because the acts described are beyond anything you could ever imagine one human being doing to another or because you care about the person she is accusing and can't imagine that person doing such a thing—it is vitally important that you work on believing her. Survivors desperately need to know that others believe their story, even if they sometimes doubt themselves or have only vague memories.

And so, if you believe that the survivor is telling the truth, tell her so. If you have suspected that there was something going on that wasn't quite right for some time now, tell her about your suspicions. If you have secretly wondered whether you were also abused by the same person, say so. This is not the time to decide you are not going to get involved or to take sides. The survivor needs to be believed, and if you do believe her, don't deprive her of this gift.

Tell her it was not her fault.

Most survivors blame themselves in some way for the abuse. They blame themselves for being somewhere they weren't supposed to be, for not telling, for the abuser's arousal, for taking their daddy away from their mommy. Even though they are told time and time again by their therapist, by books on childhood sexual abuse, and by those in their support groups that they were absolutely blameless when it comes to the abuse, they still don't believe it. They need to hear it from their family, those they feel will blame them the most. They need to hear from you that you know they did not cause the abuser to become aroused no matter how much they wiggled on his lap, that no child has the power to steal a husband away from his wife, that sex between an older sibling and a younger one is sexual abuse, or that just because they didn't tell didn't mean they wanted the abuse to continue. They need to hear all this and more—more encouragement, more support, and more understanding—from you, their family.

Recognize what part you had (or didn't have) in allowing the sexual abuse to occur or in causing the difficulties between you.

FOR PARENTS

Although the responsibility for the sexual abuse itself is always the perpetrator's, parents are often unwitting collaborators who can set the stage for the abuse in a number of ways. The following items are not to be viewed as accusations but rather as a way for you to begin to understand why the survivor in your family may be angry with you. By recognizing and then acknowledging your part in the abuse or in the family's being dysfunctional, you can make a tremendous contribution to both the survivor's recovery and the recovery of the entire family.

Did you make it possible for your child to be sexually abused in any of the following ways?

BY DENYING YOUR CHILDREN ATTENTION AND AFFECTION.

This caused the children in the family to be vulnerable to someone who could exploit their needs.

BY LEAVING YOUR CHILDREN UNSUPERVISED—OR POORLY SUPERVISED—FOR LENGTHY PERIODS OF TIME.

It takes time to molest a child. It takes time to prepare, coax, bribe; it takes time to earn trust. It takes time to get clothes off, fondle, penetrate, ejaculate.

BY LEAVING YOUR CHILDREN WITH CARETAKERS WHO WERE ABUSIVE, EMOTIONALLY DISTURBED, OR NEGLECTFUL.
You may have been unaware of or unwilling to see the caretaker's nature and unwittingly contributed to the abuse each time you left your children with that person. Some survivors even report that they were left with caretakers who were obviously alcoholic or emotionally disturbed and incapable of looking after children.

BY ABUSING YOUR CHILDREN PHYSICALLY, VERBALLY, OR EMOTIONALLY.
When parents don't value their children, there is little possibility of their children learning to value themselves. This makes it easier for a child molester to talk them into doing almost anything.

BY IGNORING OBVIOUS SIGNS OF ABUSE AND CRIES FOR HELP.
Parents of childhood sex-abuse victims are often so wrapped up in their own problems that they simply do not "see" their children at all, or they may be protecting themselves from the awareness of their own child-hood abuse. In addition, not noticing the abuse protects them from having to take some action to stop it. A mother often does not notice the warning signs because she doesn't want to have to leave her husband. Grandparents have been known to turn a blind eye to abuse because they don't want to have to confront their son or daughter.

BY MAKING YOUR CHILD FEEL THAT YOU WOULDN'T BELIEVE HER IF SHE TOLD.
Your child may have consistently had the experience of telling you something that was true, only to be told that she was making it up or exaggerating. As one survivor put it, "I didn't tell my mother about the sexual abuse because I assumed she would call me a liar like she always did when I tried to tell her what was going on in our family."

BY SHOWING OTHER PEOPLE THAT YOU DID NOT VALUE YOUR CHILDREN.
Some parents have such disdain for their children that they believe they deserve to be mistreated and abused. One client, who was repeatedly sexually and physically abused by her baby-sitters, told me, "They saw how my mother felt about me, and so they treated me with disgust like she did. If your own mother doesn't care about you, then why should others?"

BY MAKING YOUR CHILD FEEL THAT YOU COULDN'T OR WOULDN'T PROTECT HER OR HIM.
Some parents feel as helpless and powerless as their children do and therefore do not believe there is anything they can do about the abuse. If, for example, the women in your family felt powerless against the men, they probably allowed the men to do whatever they wanted to themselves and their children. In this sense, you taught your children to feel powerless around men. If both you and your mate felt powerless when it came to your parents, you may have allowed your parents to molest your children just as they may have molested you when you were a child.

FOR SIBLINGS

If you are the sibling of someone who claims to have been molested as a child, it is not unusual for you, too, to feel tremendously guilty. It is in fact common for siblings to feel responsible or guilty concerning the abuse, for several reasons:

- If you knew it was going on, you may feel that you should have told and that your telling may have in fact stopped the abuse
- You may secretly have breathed a sigh of relief each time the perpetrator chose to abuse your sibling and not you
- You may have been jealous of the attention the perpetrator gave your sibling. You may have even thought the sexual behavior was a special thing they shared and you did not

- You may have been so angry at your sibling (because you were jealous of her, because you didn't get along, because she was abusive to you) that you felt she deserved the sexual abuse.

Whatever your reason for feeling guilty, it is important for you to realize that as a child yourself, you were in no way responsible for your sibling. No matter how much older you were or how much responsibility or authority your family gave you over your sibling, you were in fact just a child yourself and therefore not responsible for what happened to your sibling or any other child. The sooner you become clear about this, the better you will be able to support your sibling in her recovery.

Apologize to the survivor for what you have done to hurt her.

FOR PARENTS

It is very important for the recovery of the survivor and for your own healing that you be willing to apologize to your child for anything you did to set her up for the abuse or for any way that you have not supported her since she told you about the abuse. While this may be very difficult for you to do, this acknowledgment and apology will do more for your child than you could ever imagine and will in turn do more in terms of healing your relationship than anything else you can do. This is what Jennifer had to say:

"When my mother told me that she was sorry she had not protected me better, and that she realized she should have never married my stepfather and brought him into our lives, I just broke down and sobbed. I felt so good that finally she was able to recognize what she had done, how she had endangered me by bringing an alcoholic and a sex addict into our lives. That was all I had really needed from her for the past five years, just for her to admit what she'd done and to apologize to me."

As a part of accepting responsibility for not protecting your child, tell her you should have been aware enough to see what was going on and strong enough to stand up for her. Acknowledge her feelings rather than defending yourself or the abuser.

In addition to the apology, she needs to have her perceptions validated by your telling her exactly what mistakes you made, not as an excuse but as a way of helping her understand you better. Jennifer's mother had this to say about her side of the story:

"I had felt all along that my daughter was blaming me for her stepfather abusing her. In fact, she seemed to be more angry with me than with him. I guess this made me so defensive that I couldn't really hear what she was saying. Finally, with the help of her therapist, I came to realize that in fact, I did owe her an apology for exposing her to such a man. He turned out to be an alcoholic who became extremely violent toward me (and now I have learned to her as well) when he was drinking. I didn't know this when I married him, but I realize now that there were warning signs I chose not to heed. Also, I should never have stayed with him after he beat me the first time, but I was afraid I couldn't make it on my own financially. I had five kids, and I didn't even finish high school.

"I also had to apologize to her for leaving her alone with him. But I never imagined he'd rape her! I assumed that all his anger was directed toward me. She was just a child—who would have thought a grown man would have done such a thing? Now I know better and would never leave a child alone with a man like that, but I really didn't know before. I wish I had."

Apologizing to your adult child is probably the best thing you can possibly do to help her. Your apology will feel like a wonderful gift from you, something she will always appreciate and be grateful for. It's really all she ever wanted from you concerning the sexual abuse, and your apology will help her to let go of her anger toward you.

It is important that you are sincere in your apology, however. The survivor will sense if you are not, and the whole thing will backfire on you. Don't apologize unless and until you really feel it.

Recognize that the survivor has a right to her anger toward you.

FOR NONOFFENDING PARENTS

Children look to their parents to protect them, and they have a right to expect this protection. Whether you knew about the sexual abuse or should have known about it, whether you brought someone into their life who was unsafe or didn't adequately supervise them, the fact is that you did not protect your child adequately. For this reason, your child may be very angry with you and rightfully so. Allow her to express her anger toward you as long as she does not become abusive.

Your child has the right to be angry with you for any and all of the following reasons:

- For not protecting her
- For looking the other way
- For setting her up for the abuse
- For blaming her
- For not listening when she tried to tell you
- For not believing her
- For not leaving an abusive or alcoholic man
- For not offering her the warmth, understanding, and attention that she needed.

While it will be difficult for you to listen to your loved one's anger without getting defensive, it is possible, as Melody discovered:

"By the time I finally believed my son about my brother abusing him he told me it was too late. He was so angry with me for not believing him before and for taking my brother's side that he kept pushing me away each time I tried to reach out to him. But I was determined to be the kind of supportive mother I should have been all along.

"Finally, I asked if I could go to his therapist with him. Reluctantly, he agreed. During our session, his therapist suggested I just listen while he told me how angry he was with me. This was really hard, but I managed to get through that session just listening to all the anger he had stored up. At the end of the session, my son said that he felt a lot better about me, and that made it all worthwhile."

Although your child doesn't have the right to blame you, criticize you, or yell at you—she needs to. Ideally, she needs to be given free license to do all of these things in order to get her anger out. Unfortunately, we do not live in an ideal world, and the fact is that most parents simply cannot tolerate having their own child (or anyone else for that matter) become openly angry with them. Most parents of survivors do not have very high self-esteem and feel frightened of other people's anger. This is especially true of those who come from abusive homes themselves where they experienced their own parents yelling or hitting one another or if they were abused in this way themselves. But if you can allow your adult child to confront you with her angry feelings, it will help her tremendously and will do much to help bring the family back together.

Certainly you should not tolerate abusive behavior on your adult child's part. No one has a right to abuse you, no matter what you have or have not done. If you start to feel abused, or if you just feel you aren't strong enough to handle your child's anger, you will need to tell her to stop. Tell her you wish you could listen but you just can't. Suggest that she get her anger out in another way, such as writing a letter to you that you promise to read. If she hasn't already begun therapy, suggest she do so or join a support group where she can ventilate her anger with other survivors. Tell her that you support her need to release her anger and that perhaps after she vents her anger more she won't be quite so intense and you can then listen to her better. *Tell her it's okay for her to be angry with you.* Don't punish her for it by not speaking to her or by getting back at her in some way.

Stand up for her against the perpetrator.

This may be one of the hardest things you will need to do in order to support the survivor and to bring healing to your family. It is extremely difficult to have to choose between your spouse and your child, between one child and another, one sibling and another, or a sibling and a parent, and that is what standing up against a perpetrator will feel like.

In actuality, standing up for the survivor is not really standing up against the perpetrator but *for* the family and for the truth. You are not only supporting the survivor in a very significant way by validating her perceptions and letting her know you believe her, but you are supporting the entire family—including the perpetrator—in becoming healthier. Keeping the secret of the sexual abuse has made the entire family sick. Openly exposing the secret will rob it of its potency and help to heal the entire family.

The perpetrator needs to know that others in the family know what he has done. He needs to know that he can no longer pretend that it didn't happen, that he can no longer lie about it or blame the victim for it. This is the only way that the perpetrator is going to admit what he has done and thus begin his own process of recovery. Only by confronting the perpetrator directly can the family let him know that he needs help.

Back her up in the family.

The survivor needs all the support she can get, especially from other family members. If you have come to believe her, then she will need you to tell other family members. Not only will this help her feel she is not alone but it will also help other family members to come out of denial. It is much more difficult to disbelieve two family members than one.

Ask the survivor what you can do now to support her.

FOR PARENTS

Although it is painful to realize that you did not protect your child, it will not help either of you for you to stay stuck in regret and guilt for what you didn't do before. It will do you and your child no good to continually chastise or blame yourself.

Instead, focus on what you can do now for your child, how you can help her recover from her pain. You have the opportunity to help her now in a very profound way by showing her understanding, compassion, and a willingness to admit your mistakes and change for the better.

FOR ALL FAMILY MEMBERS

No matter how much time has passed since the survivor told you about the abuse, it is never too late to support her. Start by telling her you believe her, telling other family members that you believe her, and standing up to the perpetrator with her. There may be other ways you can support her as well, ways you have never thought of. Ask her what you can do to help her in her recovery process. Ask if she needs financial assistance to help pay for her therapy; ask her if you can run errands for her when she is going through an especially difficult time. Tell her that you would be willing to go to therapy with her if it would help her but again, your offer must be sincere.

Try to understand if the survivor needs some time
away from you or the family.

During the recovery process, many survivors discover that they cannot be around some or all of their family members for a time. Often this is because the family does not believe them or is not able to confront the perpetrator with the abuse. Feeling that they have been let down by their parents or other family members is only part of the reason for wanting some distance. The most important reason is that survivors often do not trust their own perceptions and feelings when they are around those who do not believe them. This does not mean that the abuse did not occur, only that the abuse was shrouded in such secrecy and confusion that in the face of disbelief from their family, survivors tend to discount their own reality. Thus, survivors often feel that until they can firmly hold onto their reality even in the face of their family's denial, they must stay away.

Often survivors find their progress is thwarted whenever they see their parents. This is especially true if their parent or parents are still in denial about the sexual abuse or if they are especially controlling and domineering. When this is the case, the survivor may revert to being a subservient or fearful child who allows her parents to dictate how she should run her life.

Even if you believe and support your relative, she still may need some time away from you to work on her issues without interference from her family, time to separate emotionally from her family and learn to stand on her own, and time to heal from her wounds and thus be better able to reassess her family relationships.

More will be written about this in the next chapter, where I discuss the stages of recovery a survivor goes through. In the meantime, if your child or sibling has told you she needs time away, try not to see it as a punishment but rather as a necessity for her. Try to respect her wish to discontinue contact with you temporarily, and do not try to talk her out of her decision. It is based on sound reasoning and will in many circumstances help the survivor to grow stronger and heal faster.

Get help for yourself.

FOR PARENTS

You may need help in order to feel strong enough to face all the intense feelings that inevitably surface when a child discloses that she was sexually abused. You will need to recognize and express your feelings of pain, anger, guilt, shame, and fear with supportive people who understand what you are going through. Parent support groups, treatment groups for mothers and victims, educational classes on incest, and conjoint therapy with your adult child are effective in countering the experience of social stigma, guilt, and family disruption. With help, nonoffending parents in incestuous families can learn to be supportive of their children and begin to rebuild their families.

If you have never been in therapy, or do not believe that therapy really works, it will be difficult for you to take this step. It may help if you realize that therapy is not just for "crazy" or self-indulgent people. It is for those who have been traumatized, those who have come to realize that they are out of control in some area of their lives, and for those who are dedicated to growth and change in their life. If you feel that you fit one or all of these categories, you are a prime candidate for therapy. Certainly, you must realize that your family is in trouble and needs outside help to heal the wounds that the sexual abuse has created. At the end of the book I will address more of your concerns about therapy and offer suggestions on how to find a competent therapist.

FOR SIBLINGS

Often siblings of survivors need to enter counseling in order to become strong enough to back up the survivor in her dealings with other family members or to stand up to the perpetrator with her. Tammy's is a case in point:

"I knew my sister had been sexually abused by our father, but I was just too afraid of him to let anyone else in my family know. I wanted to be able to come forward, because no one else in the family believed her, but I just wasn't strong enough at the time. So I started therapy and worked on my fears of my father and on becoming more assertive. Eventually, I was able to tell my mother that I had seen my father molesting my sister, and this made all the difference in our family. My mother believed me and confronted my father, who in turn confronted me, calling me a liar. My worst nightmare had come true, but thanks to therapy I was able to stand my ground, even with my father."

Learn how the family situation contributed to the abuse.

Families where incest or sexual abuse have occurred have many things in common. Learning about these patterns will help you understand how and why the abuse occurred. It will also help you address the other important problems in your family and thus help the family to become a healthy, functional one.

For example, in addition to child sexual abuse, your family may also have a history for generations of other problems that increase the potential for incest, such as alcoholism or emotional disorders. Family patterns that allow alcoholism to continue untreated for many years also permit sexual abuse to occur undetected.

Incest families are often run in an authoritarian manner, with mother and father both adhering to limiting, stereotypical male and female roles. Children also learn roles of victim and perpetrator from watching their parents interact or by picking up on the intimidation, fear, and helplessness the nonoffending adult feels toward the perpetrator. This type of parental modeling limits the options children perceive for getting out of the abusive relationship. Many victims assume that being dominated and treated poorly by the perpetrator is just a fact of life, not something to be challenged.

In addition, in his book, *Adult Children of Abusive Parents*, Steven Farmer has outlined eight interactional elements found in all abusive families. They are:

- Denial
- Inconsistency and unpredictability
- Lack of empathy
- Lack of clear boundaries
- Role reversal
- The closed family system
- Incongruent communication
- Extremes in conflict.

127

Briefly, I will describe how these elements work together to make up the dysfunctional family system.

DENIAL. In dysfunctional families there is a consistent tendency to deny feelings and deny the truth. Everyone pretends that things are better than they actually are. Parents lie to their children and themselves so often that everyone ends up believing the lies. They constantly tell their children that what they felt, what they saw, and what they heard was wrong. This causes the children to doubt their own perceptions.

For example, in a dysfunctional family, the following scenario, with some modifications, is commonplace. The father comes home drunk and belligerent and starts an argument with the mother. As the parents yell and scream at each other, the children look on in horror. Finally, the father clenches his fist and beats the mother all over her body until she is unconscious. Then the father yells at the kids to get to sleep. The next morning the children tentatively enter the kitchen to find mother making breakfast for father. They are both acting as if nothing happened the night before. This confuses the children at first, but they are so relieved to find their mother all right and their father over his angry mood, that they join in on the denial and pretend that last night was all a bad dream. This "mass denial," like mass hysteria, is so compelling and so contagious that it feeds off itself. The more one member in the family denies the truth about what is really happening in the family, the more it encourages other members of the family to do the same. At first it just feels better not to have to face the pain of the truth, and eventually each grows to doubt his own perceptions. Everyone begins thinking that if other members of the family act as if nothing happened, then maybe nothing did. Maybe they were imagining it all along.

INCONSISTENCY AND UNPREDICTABILITY. Dysfunctional families, rather than serving as a source of stability and safety, become sources of turbulence, chaos, and danger. Rules are often unclear and often broken. Parental behavior fluctuates daily, even hourly. Children often have to guess at what their parents will do next, and they find it impossible to predict with any certainty whether their parents will be there for them at all, either physically or emotionally. Parents "forget" to pick their children up at the movies, don't come home when they are expected, and are not available to comfort their child in need.

LACK OF EMPATHY. In healthy families, parents have empathy for their children. Empathy is the ability to "walk in another person's shoes," the ability to be sensitive and responsive to another's feelings and needs. In dysfunctional families, parents do not know how to empathize with their children because their parents did not empathize with them. They have difficulty relating to the feelings and needs of their children because their own needs were denied and discounted when they were children. Because of this lack of empathy, these parents tend to punish their children too often and too severely.

LACK OF CLEAR BOUNDARIES. Each person needs to have a private space that belongs to her and her alone. This space is both physical and emotional. Our physical or territorial boundaries are the immediate space around our body. We each have a comfort zone, a given space between ourselves and others that enables us to feel comfortable, unthreatened. For example, if someone invades your space by standing too close to you, you will feel threatened and will need to back away from him. Psychological boundaries include the sense of oneself as separate from another person. Psychological boundaries develop as children gain an awareness of their physical boundaries. In functional families, each member has an awareness of both his physical and psychological self and sees himself as distinct from others in the family.

In a healthy, functional family, there are *discernible* (recognizable as distinct) boundaries between the individuals in the family; whereas in dysfunctional families, the boundaries between family members are unclear. The dysfunctional family can be likened to a large, sticky mass. Everyone in the family is emotionally "stuck" to everyone else. There is no psychological and emotional separation between one individual and another.

Privacy is seldom afforded to a child in a dysfunctional home. The parents enter the bathrooms or bedrooms without knocking, read mail addressed to their children, and listen to their children's private conversations. Respect for privacy (boundaries) is essential for personal development. Without it, children find it difficult to differentiate between themselves and the rest of the family.

In dysfunctional families, children are allowed to sleep with parents and take showers with them; parents walk around the house naked, watch their children while they take baths and use the toilet; older brothers are allowed to sleep with younger sisters. There is often an open-door policy, in which no one is allowed to close and/or lock the bathroom and bedroom doors; everything is public, allowing no privacy whatsoever.

On the other hand, in healthy families, physical and psychological boundaries are consistently respected. There are rules such as knocking before you enter a room and putting on clothes before you come out of the bedroom or bathroom. Children are taught to say no to anyone who tries to touch them when they do not want to be touched.

In dysfunctional families, children are not taught that they have any rights. In fact, their experience teaches them that adults have the right to have easy access to them. Whenever their parents want, they can reach out and hit them, grab them, or sexually abuse them. They are told to hug and kiss visitors whether they want to or not and made to feel bad if they try to refuse. Their belongings are given away, sold or thrown away without their permission or knowledge.

ROLE REVERSAL. The appropriate roles for parents in a healthy family are to protect their children, to provide guidance and support for them, to set limits when needed. In a dysfunctional family, the roles are very often reversed. Parents turn to their children to meet their needs, whether they be for support, advice, affection, or even sex. Children in these families often become "little adults" capable of running a household, taking care of younger siblings, even earning money for the family. These little adults learn to act like pseudo adults, even though they are children. They are not allowed to act like children; if they express their childlike qualities they may be abused or abandoned. In effect, these little adults never had a childhood and thus did not have a chance to develop emotionally, like children in healthy families.

CLOSED FAMILY SYSTEM. A dysfunctional family system is a closed one. Parents maintain few ties outside of the family. They do not share their home with friends or neighbors, nor are children allowed to bring friends over. There is a pervasive sense of isolation within the family, with little or no connection to anything larger than the family. This is true both because of parental refusal to allow children to socialize and because of children's embarrassment concerning the family. There are secrets to be kept. Parents do not want their children to have any ties with the outside world, for fear of their exposing physical or sexual abuse or alcoholism. Children do not want to risk the embarrassment of their friends seeing their parent drunk, or yelling at them in front of their friends.

INCONGRUENT COMMUNICATION. In dysfunctional families, parents often say one thing while their body language shows something entirely different. This makes it difficult for their children to decipher their parents' real message. Children are often confronted with mixed messages, thus having to guess what the actual message is. Confused by mixed messages, children learn not to trust what was said and instead be alert to how it was said. They become acutely aware of all the nonverbal messages their parents send, finding them to be far more reliable than their words.

EXTREMES IN CONFLICT. In a dysfunctional family, there is either too much or too little conflict. When there is too much conflict, there is often emotional and physical abuse. The atmosphere is tense, and the child

131

never knows when the next explosion will occur. Fighting becomes a way of life. Children become hypervigilant and ready for the next attack.

When there is too little conflict, everything is kept hidden. Problems and issues are never fully discussed, and no one ever fights. Problems that are never directly handled tend to fester.

Child abuse occurs almost exclusively within dysfunctional families. It is easy for abuse to flourish in an environment where there is denial, unpredictability, a lack of parental empathy toward the child, a lack of clear boundaries, role reversal, a closed family system, incongruent communication, and extremes in conflict. Sexual abuse occurs when there is denial, little or no sense of boundaries, role reversal, and a closed family system. When a parent is inconsistent and unpredictable and has little or no empathy for his child, physical abuse is common, as is neglect and abandonment. And finally, when there is strong denial in a family that is a closed system, any abusive behavior is ignored and can go unchecked.

Support the survivor through the recovery process.

The following guidelines will help you support the survivor in your family in the best possible ways thoughout the recovery process:

- Continue to learn all you can about sexual abuse and the healing process
- Allow the survivor time and space to express her anger
- Allow the survivor to blame others (including you) for a while
- Allow the survivor time and space to express her pain
- Respect the time and space it takes to heal
- Understand that you will have to earn her trust
- Don't try to rescue her or do her healing for her
- Support the survivor in her changes.

Learn all you can about sexual abuse and the healing process.

One of the best ways to support a survivor in recovery is to become aware of what she is going through. This will help you avoid misjudging her and being impatient and critical. One of the ways of gaining understanding for what a survivor is going through is to read some of the many books written on the subject of adult survivors of sexual abuse. A listing of such books is provided at the back of this book.

Armed with accurate information, you will be far more equipped to lend an ear to the survivor when she needs to talk, to be her ally against those who will tell her that she is making a big deal out of nothing, and to tolerate more of her behaviors even when they seem inconsiderate or bizarre.

Allow the survivor the time and space to release her anger.

Survivors are extremely angry people. Anyone who is victimized is seething with anger at having been violated. Survivors of sexual abuse were usually unable to express this anger at the time, either because they were afraid of the perpetrator or because they were unable to fully grasp the fact that someone they love could do this to them.

Because they repress or bury their anger, or because they deny or minimize the abuse itself, their anger becomes hidden so deeply inside that they are unaware of it until they begin working on their sexual-abuse issues. Then, because they are made aware of their anger by their therapist or other group members, because they are given permission to have their anger (perhaps for the first time), they will begin to express this pent-up anger. Often, because their anger has been building up for so long, it comes out in an explosion, bombarding anyone and everyone in its path, even someone not at all involved in the abuse. At other times it will be focused primarily on the perpetrator, a nonoffending parent, or a silent partner. We've already talked about what to do when a survivor directs her anger toward you. But you will also need help in knowing how to cope with her anger even when it is directed toward others or herself.

It is necessary for the survivor to express her anger, even if it seems inappropriate or extreme to you. You may become frightened that she is going to get in trouble with her anger because it seems to burst out at the most inopportune times, or in the form of constant conflicts with others. Laura shared with me how she was worried about her sister, Janine:

"When Janine first remembered that she had been molested by our grandfather, she started getting angry at men in general. If a guy just looked at her in a flirtatious way she became enraged. I remember one time a man made a remark to us as we walked past him. I just wanted to keep on walking and ignore the guy, but Janine stopped dead in her tracks and confronted him. They got into a big yelling match, and at one point I thought the guy was going to hit Janine. I had to practically drag her away before she got hurt. I'm afraid I won't be there next time to drag her away and she'll really get into trouble."

Even though you may be afraid for the survivor, there is little you can do to protect her from her own emotions. Nine times out of 10, survivors seem to get through the anger phase without endangering their own lives or those of others. They may bristle a lot and blow off a lot of steam, and they will undoubtedly be hard to get along with at times, but in general their anger is harmless. If they are in therapy, in a support or recovery group, or in a 12-step program, their therapist or fellow group members will encourage them to find constructive ways of releasing their anger. If the survivor is *not* in therapy or a part of a support group or 12-step program and you are concerned about the way she is handling anger, you may want to encourage her to seek outside help. Other than this suggestion, the only other thing you can do is to remind yourself that she will pass through this phase as more and more anger is released. The best way for you to help is to give her the understanding, space, and time to continue releasing her pent-up anger.

If you were raised in an environment where there was a lot of fighting, verbal or physical abuse, or a tremendous amount of chaos, you may react instantly to the survivor's display of anger. When she begins to yell, for example, you may suddenly be propelled back into your childhood and find yourself reexperiencing the verbal abuse of a parent. Although you may not consciously remember this experience, you may experience the event all over again, as if it were happening right now. You may become frightened, and your body may become numb or frozen or you may feel shaky. You may feel like crying as you reexperience the pain you felt to hear such harsh words spoken to you or someone you love. You may also feel nauseated or have a tight or upset stomach. Or you may feel angry remembering how enraged you felt with the abusive person. You may find yourself clenching your jaw, tightening your fists, or feeling tense in your shoulders. These are all signs that you are not just reacting to the survivor's angry words but to those of some significant person in your life, most likely from your childhood.

If you come from a home where there was verbal or physical abuse, you will have a very low tolerance for the expression of anger. Yelling or even harsh words will affect you more than someone who has not experienced verbal abuse, causing you to cower in fear or erupt in a rage. The slamming of doors, the hitting of fists on tables, or any other overt display of anger may frighten you more than it would someone who hasn't experienced physical violence. And certainly, hearing a survivor hitting a pillow with a tennis racket, screaming into a pillow, or any of a number of acts that survivors are encouraged to indulge in to constructively release their anger will be uncomfortable for you. If you are bothered by such displays of anger, take care of yourself by not being around the survivor during these times. But at the same time take responsibility for the fact that these are *your* reactions, based on your own personal experience, and don't make the survivor feel guilty for causing you to feel these feelings.

You may discover that you are uncomfortable with any display of anger, even when the survivor is not explosive with her anger. You will need to take responsiblity for your own discomfort and not allow it to spill over into the relationship with the survivor, making her feel like a bad person for feeling and expressing anger that she has every right to feel and express.

Perhaps you were not allowed to express your anger when you were a child or perhaps you were taught that anger is a weakness or even a sin. The expression of anger is a necessary and healthy thing, and the repression of it can cause all kinds of problems, from depression to physical ailments like ulcers and high blood pressure. While you have a right to your own beliefs about anger, you do not have the right to impose that belief on a survivor, especially when it will only cause her to feel more confused, inhibited, or angry.

In addition, remember that as a family member you are not as objective as, say, a friend might be. While a friend might be able to allow the survivor to express her feelings of anger, rage, or hatred toward the perpetrator or toward unprotective parents, you have your own interests or the interests of the family at stake. Your own need for peace in the family may override your ability to support the survivor's needs. For example, even if you believe and support your sibling, you might find yourself trying to calm her down whenever she expresses anger toward your parents. Although you might appreciate why she is angry, you may become frightened and threatened that she might alienate your parents.

The survivor is learning from her therapist, group, or program that anger is a healthy emotion and that she needs to find constructive ways of releasing it in order for her to recover from the abuse. If you tell her the opposite, either directly or indirectly (by showing signs of disapproval, for example), she may doubt what she is learning from her therapist or feel even more alienated from you. Either way, you are hindering rather than helping the survivor by imposing your beliefs on her.

Allow the survivor to blame others for a while.

Most survivors blame themselves for the abuse. No matter how often they are told it was not their fault, that they were an innocent child, that they didn't ask for it, and so on, they don't really believe it. They may understand it intellectually, but they don't believe it emotionally. For this reason, therapists encourage survivors to begin to place the blame where it belongs—on the perpetrator.

Although we all blame others, it is not something that is encouraged in our society. In fact, we are constantly being told that we should not blame others. Religious leaders, talk-show therapists, and self-help books all tell us that blaming is unhealthy for ourselves and for those we blame. While there is much to be said for this point of view and for forgiveness in general, survivors of sexual abuse need to be able to blame their perpetrators for a while to offset the burden of blame they impose on themselves. Let the survivor in your family blame those who are responsible for her pain for a while. She or he will more than likely work past the blaming stage and be far healthier for it.

Many people believe that survivors need to work toward forgiving the perpetrator and other members of their family of origin. But the issue of forgiveness is something every survivor must decide for herself.

Because you are a member of the family, you may have an investment in the survivor's forgiving the perpetrator or other family members. You may be uncomfortable with things the way they are and want there to be peace in the family once more. You may feel uncomfortable having to take sides in the family and want the survivor to forgive and forget so that you can get out of the middle. Try not to allow your needs to get in the way of what the survivor needs to do in order to take care of herself. If you push the survivor to forgive, you will be interfering with her recovery process. She doesn't need pressure from you to forgive when she may already be struggling to give herself permission to be angry. You will either cause her to be extremely confused or to distance herself or even become estranged from you because she cannot tolerate the pressure.

Forgiveness is difficult and sometimes impossible. There are many, many people who, no matter how hard they try, have been unable to forgive those who abused or neglected them so severely as children. There are some acts that are truly unforgivable, and if someone does not admit that he has done wrong, it is very difficult if not impossible to forgive him for it.

If the abuser is willing to accept responsibility for his actions and to apologize to the survivor, she may feel like forgiving him. But if the abuser refuses to admit that he caused damage and to apologize for that damage, the survivor may not feel like forgiveness is in order. In fact, some survivors have deliberately chosen *not* to forgive as a way of maintaining a needed distance from the person who abused them and as a way of guaranteeing that they will not be manipulated into a situation where they will be abused again.

Many survivors actually have a harder time withholding forgiveness than they do in forgiving. They have a tendency to forgive too quickly, often failing to consider their own needs. In an attempt to please their parents or others who say that they should forgive, they may push down their anger—anger that can actually help them to recover. Ironically, it is only after we have been able to release our anger that we are able to truly forgive.

It is not necessary for a survivor to forgive in order to recover or to go on with her life. If, during the process of recovery, she gets to the place where she can forgive, she will undoubtedly feel a sense of relief and freedom from the past. But forgiving doesn't mean that we forget or ignore the past—it just means that we no longer carry the anger from the past with us today.

Allow the survivor the time and space to feel her pain.

Survivors need plenty of time and space to cry all the tears they were never allowed to shed, to feel the pain of the betrayal and the intrusion of sexual abuse. They need to mourn the loss of their innocence, their childhood, their trust, and their self-esteem.

Once again, as with overt displays of anger, your own upbringing may influence how you react to the survivor's pain and crying. If you were scolded for crying, told that big kids don't cry, or even punished for crying, you may have internalized these injunctions and now be passing them on to others. While your parents may have had good intentions in discouraging you from crying, we have learned that crying is an extremely necessary act, one that promotes healing of both physical and emotional wounds. Don't pass on the message that it is not okay to cry.

Survivors gain strength by crying. They are not displaying weakness. They are getting healthier with each tear they shed. And don't worry, they won't cry forever—just long enough to heal their wounds.

Respect the time and space it takes to heal.

The recovery process is a long and slow one. Pressure from you to speed it up will only prolong it. Survivors already feel that there is something terribly wrong with them because they can't get over the trauma and go on with their lives like everyone always tells them to do. They already feel as if they are stupid and dense. Complaints that they aren't recovering fast enough may further damage their already low self-esteem.

Because the survivor cares about you, she cares about your opinion. Survivors tend to be easily influenced by others, so be aware that your complaints about her therapy, her therapist, the length of time it is taking, or the amount of money it is costing can cause your loved one to begin to doubt herself, her therapist, and the recovery process. Survivors already have enough difficulty learning to trust others. Don't reinforce this tendency by casting doubts on what they are doing. Your relative is working with her therapist in a joint effort to recover. Trust that she is the best judge of whether she is getting the kind of help she needs.

Often survivors are encouraged by their therapist and by members of their recovery group to do things that seem very bizarre, such as to carry around a stuffed animal, to talk out loud to an imaginary perpetrator, to write with their less dominant hand, and to color with crayons. Try to realize that there is a good reason for having survivors do these kinds of things. While you may not understand the rationale behind them, trust that the survivor is getting some benefit from them.

If your relative tends to constantly complain about her therapist or her recovery group, instead of agreeing with her or suggesting she quit, suggest she share with her therapist or with the members of her group some of her feelings. Survivors need to be encouraged to express their feelings directly to the people they are upset with so they can learn that it is safe to do so.

The only time when it would be appropriate for you to interfere with a survivor's therapy would be if you believe that she is being further victimized by an unscrupulous therapist. Unfortunately, there are therapists who use their role as authority figure to take advantage of their clients sexually. Some therapists have been known to have sex with their clients in their office and then, as if that wasn't harmful enough, to actually charge them for a visit, asserting that by having sex with their therapist, they will be able to overcome their sexual problems or fears of intimacy.

If your relative confides, or you suspect, that her therapist is becoming sexual with her in any way, let her know that she is being reabused, that what the therapist is doing is illegal, and that she needs to find another therapist. Furthermore, suggest she tell her next therapist about the situation, since she will need help to overcome this most recent abuse. Her new therapist can also help her decide if she wants to take legal action against the abusive therapist.

You may feel that therapy is not helping your relative if you see no obvious signs of improvement or if she actually seems to be getting worse. But it can take five years or more of individual and group therapy for a survivor to recover from such a devastating trauma. Sometimes the changes she makes will be very evident, and other times they will not. Just because you don't see the kinds of visible changes that you had hoped for doesn't mean that she isn't indeed recovering.

Understand that you must earn the survivor's trust.

Childhood sexual abuse destroys a survivor's ability to trust. From earliest childhood we are warned that *strangers* are dangerous, but seldom if ever are we warned about certain types of behavior, no matter who is responsible—family, friends of the family, doctors, dentists, teachers, camp counselors, or coaches. And while a child who has been attacked by a stranger can retreat to the safety of home, to be comforted by Mommy and Daddy, who is there to comfort the child when Mommy or Daddy is the abuser?

When your first sexual experience is with a sex offender, you learn some terrible things about people and about life. You learn that people will do almost anything—lie, betray their mates, and even abuse those they love in order to satisfy their own selfish needs. You learn that someone can tell you he loves you one minute and hurt you deeply the next. You learn that when someone says he is acting out of love it is often out of lust and selfishness.

Your loved one must learn to trust you all over again—trust that you love her, that you believe her, trust that you will not betray her. Ever so slowly, through experience with you, she must learn that you are truly on her side. She cannot just will herself to trust you. It will take time.

Depending on your family circumstances and how betrayed by you she feels, it may take a great deal of time for her to come to believe that you will not turn on her again or betray her trust.

It may not feel good to you to have to prove yourself to a family member. But remember that she once trusted you implicitly and you betrayed her by not believing her, by not protecting her better, by lying to her, by protecting the perpetrator, and so forth.

Of course, no one is completely trustworthy. We all have our weaknesses and faults, and you are no exception. It would be a tremendous lie and you would be doing her a great disservice by telling your relative that she can trust you completely at all times. The most truly loving approach would be to tell her the truth about yourself—the ways in which she can trust you and the ways in which she can't. For example, she may be able to trust that you'll back her up with the perpetrator but not that you won't sometimes deny how bad it was when she was growing up.

The best way to build trust, of course, will be for you to prove to the survivor in your family that she can rely on you, that you will keep your word. If you say you are going to do something, make every effort to do so. Otherwise, don't promise to do it. If you tell her that you will read a book on sexual abuse or that you will go with her to therapy or that you will give her the family album to look through, do it. Don't say that you will do these things to support her in her recovery and then not do them. This is not only cruel because it is giving her false hope, but it will seriously damage her ability to trust you. Of course, we all break our promises from time to time—that can't be helped. The point here is to avoid carelessly making promises you don't intend to keep and making false promises as a way of manipulating your relative.

Don't try to rescue the survivor.

There are two separate issues here: your tendency to want to take care of the survivor and her tendency to want you to take care of her. Neither is healthy for the survivor or for the family as a whole.

Try not to see the survivor as a weak victim but rather as the strong, courageous survivor that she is. While she needs your support and understanding, she does not need you to take care of her, take away her feelings, or tell her what to do. She has probably had enough people in her life who have tried to control her and direct her life for her. Now she needs to become more independent and trust her own ability to take care of herself.

While she may at times try to get you to take care of her as she has in the past, try not to get hooked into it. She'll need time to make the change from being a dependent, insecure person who doesn't trust her own judgment and abilites to the independent, self-assured one that she can become.

Support the survivor in her changes.

As a family member of a survivor, you have probably known her all her life. You have grown accustomed to her acting, thinking, expressing herself in particular ways. But through the recovery process, she will be making some significant changes in her behavior, her attitudes and beliefs, and her ways of expression. These changes may be subtle or they may be very obvious. In either case, the survivor will be different from the person you have always known her to be. Don't be surprised if she is more assertive, more expressive of her feelings and desires, more direct in her communication, more confrontational and outspoken when she doesn't like things. And don't be surprised if you find that you initially have a difficult time accepting these changes. In fact, you may find that you don't like your relative as much as you did before. You may find her too aggressive, opinionated, and outspoken, or conversely, she may seem to be more distant and less willing to share her feelings with you. Whatever changes the survivor in your family makes, you may secretly wish that she was back to being her old self. You may long for the way things used to be in the family, before the abuse was exposed.

While it is natural to feel this way, sharing such feelings with the survivor will not be helpful to her. She has worked long and hard to make important changes in her life, to become more assertive, to speak up when she doesn't like things, to value her opinions, and to make her needs known to her family and others. These changes will almost guarantee that she will not be victimized by anyone again, especially by anyone in the family.

We all tend to be threatened by change, particularly when it involves those closest to us. Instead of telling the survivor that you don't approve of her changes or that you liked her better before, share with her that you are threatened by her changes and that you are having a difficult time adjusting to them. In this way you are taking responsibility for your own difficulties and not blaming her for your reaction. You are also keeping the lines of communication open, enabling both of you to work through this difficult time of adjustment.

The suggestions made in this chapter will help you change the way you treat the survivor in your life. Although all this may seem like a lot of work, you will be rewarded with more closeness and harmony in the family, as well as the knowledge that you have substantially helped someone you love. In addition, by supporting the survivor, you are also helping the entire family heal from the devastating wounds of childhood sexual abuse, and helping yourself come out of denial about your own past and about your own family of origin.

Now that you know what the survivor needs from you, you can apply that knowledge to the various stages of recovery, which will be outlined in the next chapter. In addition, I will offer you even more specific ways of supporting the survivor during each recovery stage.

9

WHAT TO EXPECT: PHASES IN RECOVERY

U nless you know what to expect, the recovery process for survivors of childhood sexual abuse can be extremely confusing and unsettling. For example, those who are unprepared for changes in the survivor may think that their relationship with her is falling apart instead of realizing that the relationship is likely to get worse before it gets better.

During the course of their recovery, survivors will go through different stages necessary for their healing. At times they will be extremely angry and lash out at anyone around them. At other times they will be extremely depressed and withdrawn, unable to communicate how they are feeling to even those closest to them. They will inevitably go through a time where they are mourning their childhood and feeling the pain of the abuse, and because of this they may have long periods during which they cry constantly.

Because family members have their own stake in the survivor's recovery, it is understandable that you will want to know what the recovery process entails. In addition, having already withstood emotional outbursts, depression, and often rejection, many family members want to know how much change they can reasonably expect and how long it will take for it to occur.

While it is important to remember that each survivor is a unique person, most survivors go through certain predictable phases during the recovery process. Not every survivor will go through every stage at the same pace or in the order in which they are listed here. Instead, they will go through each stage in their own time.

Stage One: Facing the Truth

In this first phase, survivors begin to face the fact that they were sexually abused. They may not have specific memories yet—only a vague inner "knowing" or a strong suspicion. They may recognize that they exhibit many of the symptoms of survivors of childhood sexual abuse; they may have been told that someone else in their family was sexually abused and fear that the perpetrator may have abused them too, or they may have flashes of memory or nightmares that indicate sexual abuse. They may recently have begun to notice sexual problems; to suffer unexplained pain in their vagina, penis, or anus; to wake up at the same time every night; or to be afraid to go to sleep.

Acknowledgment is the first major sign of recovery, for only when survivors admit that they were abused can they begin to heal. Unfortunately, facing the fact that they were sexually abused as children is a painful and difficult step. Typically, survivors will go in and out of denial, being convinced one moment that they were indeed abused only to change their mind minutes, hours, or days later. They will constantly doubt their own perceptions and their memories, fluctuating between believing in them and thinking that they are making it all up in their minds. As a way of protecting yourself or another family member, you may be tempted to interpret these fluctuations as evidence that the abuse did not in fact occur. But do not give in to this inclination. Remind yourself that this is a natural part of the recovery process, and trust that your relative will eventually be able to trust her memories and stand firm with her convictions.

During this phase, survivors will be focused on bringing forth memories to validate their suspicion, perhaps by going back into their past and trying to remember their childhood through old photographs, by returning to houses they used to live in, or by talking to family members.

If the perpetrator was a family member, or someone the survivor loved or was especially close to, she will find it especially hard to admit the abuse. By far the greatest damage caused by childhood sexual abuse is the child's feeling of betrayal when she is abused by someone she loves. The resulting lack of trust, inability to get close to others, and confusion regarding her feelings toward the perpetrator can last a lifetime. Especially when the perpetrator is a parent, the child is torn between feelings of love, loyalty, and dependence and feelings of anger, fear, and betrayal.

During this time of remembering, survivors will also have to face the truth about their family of origin. This may of course mean that the survivor in your family will be facing things about you personally, so you will need to be prepared and try to be as honest with her as possible, instead of becoming defensive.

Needless to say, this will be a very difficult time for survivors, as they face what they have tried all their lives to forget. If they are able to remember the abuse itself, they will feel retraumatized by their memories and will be facing feelings that they may not have been capable of feeling at the time. Feelings of pain, fear, shame, guilt, and anger will surface as they once again experience the devastation of being violated and of feeling utterly alone with their pain and fear.

Many will go through a period of mourning as they give up the fantasy that they had a "wonderful" childhood or that they came from a healthy, normal family. They will also have to mourn the loss of their innocence, their lost childhood, and the fantasy that the perpetrator truly cared about them. Thoughout this first phase, the survivor will experience periods of moodiness, crying spells, and depression.

When she is able to admit the truth to herself, she may move into another phase of needing to tell others. It may seem to you that she has to tell *everyone*, and this may embarrass you or make you feel angry. You may hate it that she is telling everyone what you consider to be "family business," especially if the perpetrator is someone within the family.

Or she may need to tell you her story time after time until you feel tired of hearing it. Try to be patient by realizing that it is the telling of her story that makes the experience real for her. Each time she tells her story, it becomes more and more real to her, and she is able to feel more of the emotions attached to the experience.

STAGE TWO: RELEASING THE ANGER

As mentioned earlier, once the survivor has come out of denial and begins to face the truth about the abuse, about the perpetrator, and about her family of origin, she will inevitably become angry. While she will continue to feel tremendous pain and grief thoughout the recovery process, the emotion that will have the strongest impact on her recovery and be her strongest ally will be her anger.

The more a survivor faces the truth, the more angry she will become. She has the right to feel angry at any and all of the following people:

- The perpetrator
- Her parents
- Other members of her family of origin who didn't protect her
- Anyone who exposed her to the abuser
- Anyone who excused or protected the abuser
- Anyone who should have been concerned but didn't act
- Anyone who didn't believe her when she tried to tell
- Anyone who told her to forget it or told her it wasn't any big deal
- Anyone who blamed her
- Anyone who told her that she wanted it or that she did it for her own pleasure.

Most survivors seem to start by focusing their anger on the parent who did not protect them. This is probably because they are still so intimidated by the perpetrator, but it is also because survivors often feel just as betrayed by the nonprotective parent. They may focus their anger on the nonprotective parent for months and even years—especially if this parent continues to protect the perpetrator or refuses to believe the abuse occurred—before they move on to direct their attention to the perpetrator.

Eventually, the survivor will need to focus her anger on the perpetrator in order to complete her recovery. This is a very difficult phase for most survivors for several reasons: (1) the very person who abused them may have been the only one who paid them any attention; (2) they may still be afraid of the abuser; (3) they may still blame themselves for the abuse. By the time survivors have worked past these roadblocks to their free expression of anger, they are well on the road to recovery.

Don't be surprised if the survivor starts pounding the bed with a tennis racket or a foam or plastic bat, tearing up telephone books, putting her head in a pillow and screaming, or going to the garage and stomping on aluminum cans. These and many other anger-releasing techniques are recommended to survivors as healthy, constructive ways of releasing pent-up anger.

The best support you can provide a survivor during Stage 2 is to let her know that she has a right to her anger and encourage her to find constructive ways of releasing it. As mentioned in the previous chapter, you will need to allow her the time and space to release her anger and not try to talk her out of it or make her feel like a bad person for being angry.

STAGE THREE: CONFRONTING THE PERPETRATOR AND ANYONE ELSE WHO CONTRIBUTED TO THE DAMAGE

At some point in their recovery—usually after they have acknowledged they were victims and released some of their anger—survivors will need to confront those who damaged them as children: the perpetrator, the silent partner, and any other family member who either set them up for the abuse or did nothing to stop it. Whether they choose to confront directly or indirectly, most survivors experience tremendous satisfaction when they stand up to those who hurt them and express their anger and pain.

Confronting is different from releasing anger in that the purpose is for survivors to stand up to those who hurt them, not so much in an angry fashion but in an assertive one. In fact, survivors are encouraged to ventilate their anger before they confront so that they can communicate their feelings in a strong, clear, self-assured manner instead of exploding and losing control.

Survivors are also encouraged to rehearse their confrontation or at least plan what they are going to say. Generally speaking, it is recommended that the survivor include the following in her confrontation:

1. Exactly what the person did to them that caused them damage.
2. What effect the person's actions (or inaction) had on them, and how their life has been affected.
3. What they would have wanted from the person at the time.
4. How they feel about the person now and what they want from them now.

Many survivors are still too afraid of the perpetrator to confront him directly, and this may be wise. Some perpetrators are still so abusive that the survivor might be endangering herself if she were to confront face-to-face. On the other hand, many gain a tremendous sense of personal power when they do stand up to someone they have been afraid of all their life.

If a face-to-face confrontation is impossible or too threatening, survivors can write and then mail a letter, tape-record their thoughts and then send or give the tape to the person, or confront on the telephone. Other survivors choose not to involve the perpetrator or family member directly. Instead, they have an indirect confrontation through role-playing with someone who portrays the perpetrator or family member, or by writing a letter or making a tape recording without giving it to the other party.

Whatever method the survivor uses to confront those who have damaged her, the results will generally be the same. She will feel empowered, less like a victim, and less likely to allow anyone to abuse her again. She will be proud of herself for having made the confrontation, and this pride will carry over to other aspects of her life. Having completed some of her unfinished business with those from her past, she may now feel more like dealing with issues that have been building up inside her concerning her present relationships. She may choose this time to confront you about behavior she feels is abusive or unloving, and she may begin to assert her needs and desires far more often than she ever did before.

In order to support your relative during this stage, you will need to respect her enough to trust that she is the best one to decide just whom, when, and how to confront. She does not need you to protect her or do her confronting for her; nor does she need you to tell her how to go about it. Try to keep your judgments to yourself so that you don't influence her in this important decision. As a family member you may have an investment in the survivor's *not* confronting another family member. While it is natural for you to feel protective of yourself or other family members, be aware that by trying to prevent confrontation you may be hindering not only the survivor's recovery but also that of the entire family.

STAGE FOUR: RESOLVING FAMILY RELATIONSHIPS

Survivors have two major tasks to accomplish with respect to their family of origin: the resolution of intense feelings and the establishment of new boundaries with old family members. Resolving the intense, leftover feelings from the abuse allows the survivor to move on to create better relationships. Feelings such as anger, fear, betrayal, and sadness need to come to the surface and be expressed in safe, supportive ways. This can occur directly when family members are willing to be involved in a supportive way. Often, though, it is better for it to occur indirectly through therapy, either because other family members are not available or supportive or because negative consequences might ensue for the survivor. This letting go of old feelings frees the survivor from the victim role she may have played in the family and allows her to live a life unencumbered by continual bitterness and hatred.

After the survivor has confronted the perpetrator and/or members of her family of origin, some kind of resolution is called for so that she can go on with her life. A survivor may choose to reconcile with family members, or she may decide to temporarily separate from them or even "divorce" them. Her choice should be solely up to her and should not be influenced by you or anyone else. She will make this decision by determining which relationships are healthy and which are not, by confronting family members and opening up the lines of communication, and by learning healthier, more assertive ways of communicating.

Many survivors decide on temporary separation from their childhood family during the recovery process. If your relative has decided to take time out from one or more members of the family in order to facilitate her recovery, you should allow her to do so and not insist that she defend her actions. As a family member, you may feel you know what is best for the survivor and the rest of the family. You may believe that what she is doing is wrong or that she has no right to hurt other family members in such a way. But you must trust that the survivor knows what is best for her and that she must put her own needs ahead of the rest of the family's in this case.

If you are the person the survivor is needing to temporarily separate from you will probably feel intense pain. But in spite of your pain, you must resist pressuring her to change her mind. You must not try to make her feel guilty or threaten to end the relationship yourself. Try to allow yourself to feel the pain of the separation—don't cover it up with anger or resort to manipulation or threats. The most supportive thing you can do in this case is to allow the survivor her time away from you and to trust that she will come back when she is ready.

There is no prescribed duration for a temporary separation. Each survivor must decide on her own how much time she needs. Some stay away only a few months, others for years. Some break completely, having no contact whatsoever with their parents or family, while others either limit the time they spend with them or communicate only by mail or telephone. Some survivors limit their time with their family to important functions such as weddings, funerals, or anniversaries or important holidays.

A survivor's decision to "divorce" her parents or other family members may be the only alternative when the relationship is so destructive that she must choose between her health and her family. Being around family members who deny that the sexual abuse ever occurred, who accuse the survivor of lying or exaggerating, or who continue to protect the perpetrator can be extremely damaging to the survivor and can get in the way of her recovery.

Permanent separation is usually the only healthy choice for a survivor if family members do the following:

- If they continue to abuse her physically, sexually, or emotionally, and she is still unable to stand up for herself or her attempts to stop the abuse haven't worked
- If they continue to deny that she was sexually abused, persist in protecting the perpetrator, or blame her for the abuse
- If they continue to make her doubt her perceptions, memory, or sanity
- If they abuse the survivor's children or will not protect them from someone who is abusive
- If they are emotionally disturbed or are practicing alcoholics or drug addicts and refuse to get help
- If having contact interferes with the survivor's recovery or her progress in therapy.

Naturally, if the survivor does choose to divorce herself from a family member, she, too, will experience pain and loss. Even those who haven't seen their relatives in a long time have considerable difficulty permanently severing the ties. If the survivor has not already entered therapy or joined a support group, encourage her to do so before she attempts this momentous task, or encourage her to read my book *Divorcing a Parent*.

Some survivors, on the other hand, are able to successfully reconcile with their parents and other members of their family of origin. But they must first give themselves permission to limit family contact, and possibly change the entire nature of that contact, if that's what will help them affirm their strength and separateness. Some survivors choose to reconcile after they have gained assertiveness and self-protection skills, learned to reduce their expectations of how much closeness is possible, and lessened their need for love and support from their family of origin. Either because they were able to get strong enough to stand up for themselves with their family or because their family has adequately changed, they may then be willing to try one more time to connect with their families in a meaningful way.

The best way to support a survivor during this stage is to allow her to resolve her relationships with you and other family members in the way that feels best to her—not that she do what *you* think is best.

STAGE FIVE: SELF-DISCOVERY

During this phase, survivors will need to focus on discovering who they are, as distinct from their family and from the perpetrator. Because they had little if any opportunity during their childhood and adolescence to develop their own identity or sense of self, they must backtrack and do this now.

One of the best ways of discovering who we are is to focus on our feelings. Unfortunately, most of us seldom do this. Survivors are especially used to numbing themselves to their feelings, blocking out their emotions, and busily avoiding them at all costs.

The survivor will need a lot of time alone in order to increase her self-awareness and her self-knowledge. She will need permission to discover her values, beliefs, priorities, likes and dislikes, and her emotions. As she does so, she may seem terribly preoccupied. She may spend a great deal of time writing in her journal, going for long walks, or just lying in bed staring into space. As difficult as it might be for you, try to allow the survivor all the time she needs alone. This is by far the best way to support her in her self-discovery process. Reassure her that you care and that you are available to talk if she needs to.

STAGE SIX: LEARNING SELF-CARE

Learning to take care of themselves is not easy for survivors. Most either neglect themselves terribly, even to the point of being self-destructive, or focus too much of their time on taking care of others to the detriment of themselves. Survivors are often more comfortable being care-givers than care-receivers, they may have difficulty asking for what they need, or receiving a gift or a compliment. They may sacrifice their own needs, expecting to be appreciated and revered for their unselfish, generous natures.

During this phase, survivors begin to acknowledge how very important their own needs are. They learn to put their own needs first at times, instead of always taking care of others'. They learn to value themselves more by taking better care of their bodies or by respecting their privacy and boundaries and insisting that others do the same. They begin to give themselves the nurturing, encouragement, and praise that they never received as children. And they learn to be more assertive and to ask for what they want, to say no to what they don't want, and to recognize their choices and rights. Many survivors discover for the first time that they have a right to express their feelings, opinions, and needs and to make their own decisions.

Most survivors were never taught to take care of themselves in these ways. Instead, they were taught to take care of the perpetrator's or their parents' needs. Because they grew up hearing things like "Stop thinking of yourself all the time!" or "You're just a selfish brat!" they came to equate taking care of their own needs with selfishness. When they weren't being given this kind of verbal message, they were receiving non-verbal ones such as "I can't meet your needs; I have too many of my own" or "I didn't get my needs met when I was a child, so you have to take care of me now." Because of these verbal and nonverbal messages, survivors learned to sacrifice themselves for the sake of others.

You can support the survivor during this time by encouraging her to take care of her own needs first. If this is difficult for you, remind yourself that you'll have a better chance of establishing a healthy relationship if she is able to take care of her own needs.

STAGE SEVEN: SELF-FORGIVENESS

Survivors of childhood sexual abuse feel tremendous guilt and shame: for the abuse itself and for harmful things they have done to themselves and others as a result of the abuse. These feelings of guilt and shame often cause them to abuse their bodies with food, alcohol, drugs, ciga-rettes, or self-mutilation; to become accident-prone; to sabotage their success; or to elicit punishment or mistreatment from others.

For this reason, self-forgiveness is one of the most important steps in the recovery process. A survivor may have been told over and over by her therapist, members of her support group, or by you that the sexual abuse was not her fault, and she may know this on a rational, intellectu-al level. But deep down inside, she probably still blames herself for her involvement in the abuse—for being submissive or passive, for not telling anyone, for her body's response.

The process of self-forgiveness will take a long time and actually occurs during the entire recovery process. It involves learning that we cannot be held responsible for so-called choices unless they are *free* choices. A free choice is made when we understand the consequences of our actions and are not coerced, bribed, intimidated, or threatened into satisfying someone else's needs. Children and adolescents are not old enough to make a free choice to have sex with a perpetrator.

Another important aspect of self-forgiveness is learning to differentiate between what we are responsible for and what we aren't. Children are never responsible for any aspect of the sexual abuse itself. By the same token, a sexually abused child should not be held responsible for her own abusive behavior since it is more than likely a reaction to the abuse she sustained. The issue becomes less clear cut, however, with respect to the abusive behavior of an adolescent survivor. While we tend not to consider an adolescent as responsible for her behavior as an adult, if an adolescent survivor sexually abuses a younger child as a consequence of her own abuse, she does have some responsibility for her behavior. And certainly, she is responsible for her behavior as an adult, whether it be stealing, abusing her children, or driving under the influence of alcohol or drugs. Even if her behavior was clearly a result of the sexual abuse, she is still accountable for it. This means she may need to make amends to those she has hurt before she can be relieved of her guilt. She may need to go to those she has harmed, admit to them that what she did was wrong, apologize, and make restitution in the best way possible. For example, if she has stolen money, she will need to repay it. If the person she hurt needs therapy as a result of her actions, she should offer to pay for it if she can. These acts will help her begin to forgive herself for harming others.

In order for survivors to recover, they must come to terms with both their innocence and their guilt. This means forgiving themselves for those things they had no responsiblity for, holding themselves accountable for those things they were responsible for.

The best way to support a survivor during this stage is to refrain from insisting that she "forgive and forget." Forgiving the abuser or other family members is not always possible and is certainly not necessary for recovery. Survivors do need to forgive themselves, though, in order to recover.

Recovering from childhood sexual abuse can be a long and painful process. While it is inevitable that you and the survivor will go through difficult times as she recovers, understanding the recovery process can make it a lot easier for both of you.

Don't underestimate the effect you still have on your relative. Your steady, consistent support can make all the difference to her. Her emotions may be intense and difficult to understand, but simply allowing her to be whoever she is may be the best way you can support her through this difficult time.

PART III

BRINGING THE FAMILY BACK TOGETHER

Many, many families have been torn apart because of childhood sexual abuse. At a time when they needed each other the most, family members have turned away from one another because of their denial, fear of the truth, pride, need to be right, guilt, anger, and downright stubbornness. Because of their own pain, they have said things to one another that they never imagined they would say. They have done things to each other they never imagined they would do. Family members have stopped speaking to one another, stopped seeing one another, and even disowned one another over the issue of child sexual abuse. One by one, family members have turned against one another, refusing to admit when they are wrong, refusing to listen to one another, refusing even to be open to the possibliity that they might have been blind.

When the family disintegrates, everyone suffers. Holidays become a time of tension or loneliness and pain as family gatherings and family members are missed. Important family events such as weddings, graduations, birthdays, and anniversaries are strained or avoided altogether. Children miss their grandparents, aunts, uncles, and cousins, and these relatives do not get the pleasure of watching the children in the family grow up.

But there is almost always hope for reconciliation. Time, individual growth, and personal recovery can eventually mend broken alliances. Love, putting your own needs aside for a while for the sake of the family, and having empathy for everyone's position and struggle can eventually bring almost any family back together, no matter how much pain, betrayal, and anger each member of the family has felt.

10

How to
RECONCILE WITH
YOUR FAMILY

For the Survivor

This chapter does not apply to all survivors who are estranged from their family but to those who have decided, after some time away, that they are now ready to try again. It is only for those survivors who feel they are now strong enough to reconnect with their family and still maintain a sense of self. It is for those who feel they can reestablish a relationship with their family without becoming confused about the abuse or sacrificing their recovery.

It is not for those of you whose family is so dysfunctional and so abusive that a reconciliation would cause you emotional or physical harm. If anyone in your family is still exhibiting the following behaviors, it may not be safe for you to try to reconcile:

- Overt or covert sexual innuendos or looks, inappropriate sexual language or jokes, seductiveness or flirtatious behavior, or intrusive or inappropriate body language or touches
- Threatening comments or physically abusive behavior
- Inappropriate sexual behavior toward your children
- Any behavior that shows a lack of protectiveness toward your children.

In short, if someone in your family continues to exhibit behavior toward you or toward your children that is emotionally, physically, or sexually abusive, it is not advisable for you to attempt reconciliation with that person. It is vitally important that you realize an *untreated* child molester (one who has *not* undergone psychotherapy or a treatment program for sex offenders) will continue to sexually abuse children. Your children are not safe around your perpetrator if he has not received such help.

Most adult children who have divorced their parent(s), another relative, or their entire family have a secret dream of getting back together and working things out. Even though they knew at the time that divorce was the healthiest choice they could make, after some time apart, many adult children know they still love their family and long for a reconciliation, as Jeremy did:

"I felt very good about the fact that I was able to divorce my mother. I didn't do it to punish her or to manipulate her, but I was making a strong statement to her that I could not tolerate her seductiveness toward me. I didn't even speak to her for over five years and a lot happened to me in those four years. Because I wasn't around her seductiveness and because of therapy, my self-esteem improved greatly. I married a wonderful woman, and we have three children and I have a great job. Because of all this I felt good about myself and my life, and I wanted to share some of it with my mother—if she wasn't still seductive, that is. I wanted her to meet my wife and kids, and I guess there was also a part of me that wanted her to see that I was successful and had turned out well, not because of her but in spite of her.

"I guess the time away from me had changed her, too. She had aged, of course, but she seemed to have mellowed with age. And because I was now strong enough to let her know right away that I wasn't going to put up with her seductiveness, she seemed to control herself fairly well. What was equally important, though, was that when she started to slip back into her old behavior, I was able to immediately call her on it, and this would stop her dead in her tracks."

Like Jeremy, some adult children discover that being away from their parent has made them much healthier and stronger—so much so that they find they can take much better care of themselves with their parent now. Monica also gave the relationship with her parents one more try and was also successful in her attempt: "I am no longer a child around my parents," she said. "I no longer feel like their victim but their equal, and this makes all the difference."

As time passes and old wounds heal it is natural to feel more forgiving of even the most abusive parents and to miss even the most neglectful ones. Leslie, who hadn't seen or heard from either one of her parents in over seven years, found this to be true:

"Even though I don't regret divorcing my parents, I found that the more time went by, the more I was able to forgive them for the way they had treated me. And as more time passed, I also found that I missed them in my life. I decided to see them one more time to determine whether they had changed at all. I realized that since so much time had passed, I probably had forgotten how cruel they could be and how terrible I felt around them. I knew there was a risk that out of missing them I had emphasized their positive qualities in my mind. But I had to find out. I saw my reconciliation attempt as giving me a chance to see the truth—whatever it might be.

"I was pleasantly surprised by their response when I called. My mother sounded elated and called out to my father, who, much to my surprise, got on the phone immediately. I heard none of the old bitterness in his voice. Instead, I heard a genuine concern as he asked me how I was. We agreed to get together in a few weeks.

"I was very nervous as I got ready to go see them. The long car drive gave me plenty of time to review both my life with them and the years of being apart. I hadn't forgotten what they had done, but I wanted to see if things could be different.

"When my mother opened the door, she looked so happy to see me it made me cry. We hugged each other, and it felt really good. I noticed my dad in the background, looking uncomfortable and rather shy, very unlike how I had always remembered him—as an imposing figure, always angry and gruff. Seven years had aged him tremendously. He didn't look so threatening now at all. I approached him and stuck out my hand. He looked very nervous but tentatively took my hand for just a second or two. I looked him straight in the eye, and I noticed that he couldn't look at me in return. He looked really ashamed. I realized that he had not looked me in the eye since he first began sexually molesting me.

"While we talked that afternoon, I realized that in the years that we had been apart I had grown up and that I was no longer afraid of them. I talked to them as their equal, not as a frightened little child. It also became evident that they had had plenty of time to realize just how much they had damaged me. My mother cried often, telling me how much she had missed me and how she regretted so many things, most especially the fact that she had not believed me when I had told her my father had molested me. But she also told me that she was finally able to confront him about my accusation and that he had admitted to her that he had indeed abused me. I looked over at him and he nodded his head and said, 'Yes, I told her the truth. I did molest you, and I am sorry. I'm sorry I didn't admit it much earlier.'"

It is not necessary for you to forgive your parent or other family member in order to reconcile with him. You may not be ready or able to forgive by the time you are ready to attempt a reconciliation. Perhaps during the reconciliation process itself, you may obtain enough trust and healing to be able to forgive, as Annie experienced:

"I hadn't really forgiven my mother for not believing me when I told her about being molested, nor had I forgiven her for not protecting me as a child, but I decided I really wanted to try to make a go of our relationship one more time. She had finally divorced my father, so I didn't have to worry about my daughter, Kristin, being around him. She told me she was sorry for not being a better mother and she wanted to be a good grandmother to Kristin.

"It took some time, but eventually I began to trust her with my daughter, and with my own feelings. She really had changed. Even though in some ways it hurt to see her giving to my daughter in ways she never could with me, it also helped me to trust her. I began to open up to her and tell her more about the abuse, and much to my surprise, she was able to listen—not for long, usually, but long enough for me to feel like she really cared."

Some people never forgive, even though they reconcile with their relative. How can this be? It is possible to love someone for his good qualities in spite of what he has done to hurt you. In addition, some people are able to forgive the person even though they can't forgive the act.

For example, Stacey felt that she could never truly forgive her father for sexually abusing her because each time he asked for her forgiveness when she was a child, he turned around and molested her again. But he was getting old and had already suffered one heart attack. Stacey wanted to reconcile with her father before he died. This is what she told me in one of our sessions:

"I want to have some contact with my dad before he dies because I know I'll miss him when he's gone. He hurt me a lot by molesting me, but he also did some really good things for me. He was loving and kind, and he always encouraged me to be the best I could be. Don't get me wrong, I don't trust him as far as I could throw him, but he does have some goodness in him, and I want to experience that again before he dies."

You are the only one who can decide whether the time is right for forgiveness or reconciliation. Trust your instincts, follow your heart, and do not allow circumstances or other people to pressure you into a premature decision.

The Decision to Reconcile

While many survivors long for reconciliation with estranged family members, some insist on remaining divorced, as Jeannie did:

"I've tried to understand that my mother has low self-esteem because she was also sexually abused. I know she doesn't believe she can make it on her own without my stepfather and that no other man will want her, but I still have the hardest time understanding how she could stay with a man who sexually abused his own stepdaughter. As far as I am concerned, he is scum and I don't want anything to do with him—or with her, for that matter."

Jeannie certainly had reason to be angry with her mother, and she had a right to remain estranged from her, but she was nevertheless depriving herself of the mother she loved very much. Survivors like Jeannie need to distinguish between not seeing a family member because it is *unhealthy* for them and remaining estranged because they need to punish, maintain their pride, be right, or have the last word.

In Jeannie's case, she came to realize that she missed her mother very much and was suffering more from not seeing her than she would if she swallowed her pride and agreed to see her. It wasn't as if Jeannie's mother doubted her word. She believed that her husband had abused her. In fact, *he* had even admitted it, although he refused to apologize. Consequently, Jeannie did not risk becoming confused or doubting her perceptions or memory by being around her mother. Neither did she have to see her stepfather in order to see her mother. Her mother agreed to come to Jeannie's house or to meet her in a neutral place. What Jeannie's mother was unwilling and probably unable to do was to leave her husband, Jeannie's perpetrator.

Finally, Jeannie realized that she really had nothing to gain and everything to lose by not seeing her mother. She had no children to protect and while she still didn't approve of her mother's decision to stay with her stepfather, she stopped thinking of it as her mother choosing her stepfather over her and began to view it more as a symptom of her mother's low self-esteem.

Before you attempt a reconciliation, ask yourself the following questions:

- Am I strong enough to be around my relative without losing too much ground in my recovery, becoming confused about the sexual abuse, or allowing him to abuse me?

- Has my relative changed in some significant way? Is he willing to go into therapy with me or separately? Is he willing to work on a new relationship?
- Am I being pressured into a reconciliation (by other family members, by my spouse, by guilt, or by my religious beliefs) before I'm actually ready?
- Is my relative ready to reconcile with me? Or is he still angry with me for blaming him, for being angry with him, for bringing the secret out into the open, for not having seen him for a while, or for divorcing him? (If so, he may need more time to heal and to forgive, no matter how forgiving *you* might feel.)

If you can't answer yes to questions 1, 2, and 4 and no to question 3, you may want to wait a while before attempting a reconciliation.

When Brenda asked herself these questions, she realized she was not ready for a reconciliation with her brother. Although she felt she had forgiven him for molesting her when she was a child, and she wanted to put the past behind her, she realized that she still did not feel safe enough to be around him. He still looked at her seductively whenever they were together at family functions, and once he even put his hand on her behind as he passed by. When she remembered these incidents, she realized her brother had not changed sufficiently for her to be around him.

HAVE A PLAN

If you decide to attempt a reconciliation, make certain you can take care of yourself both emotionally and physically and that you will be able to retain your sense of self when you are with your relative. It is also important to realize that the only way a reconciliation can work is if all parties have undergone some significant changes. If this has not been the case, old patterns of behaving and coping are bound to reappear. These suggestions can help you to make the most of your reconciliation efforts:

1. BE REALISTIC; DO NOT EXPECT IT TO BE EASY.

Have reasonable expectations of the relationship instead of expecting everything to be different and wonderful. Otherwise, you will be disappointed and may give up before you have really started. Maureen was very realistic about her mother and her attempt at reconciliation with her:

"When I decided to try once again with my mother, I didn't expect her to be entirely different. I knew she would still have a tendency to minimize the damage I had experienced from being abused. I knew I had my work cut out for me in terms of educating her about abuse and in terms of me being patient while she learned. But she was finally willing to admit that my grandfather had molested me, and she agreed to keep him away from my children. That was at least a start."

2. DECIDE AHEAD OF TIME WHAT YOUR BOTTOM LINE IS—THAT IS, WHAT YOU EXPECT FROM YOUR RELATIVE IN ORDER FOR YOU TO BE ABLE TO RECONCILE.

For example, perhaps you are willing to forgive and forget as long as your mother is willing to tell you that she believes you were in fact sexually abused by your father (or other relative). Or perhaps you are willing to reconcile with your father (your perpetrator) if he is now willing to admit that he molested you and to enter psychotherapy.

3. MAKE SURE YOU HAVE A PLAN OF ACTION.

Do not expect things to just work out without effort on both your parts. If you have no plan, you will find that you will fall back into old behavior patterns and negative ways of communicating. Examples of such plans are:

- Investigate therapists and counseling centers who specialize in working with families of incest. Make some preliminary calls so that if your family agrees, you can all begin to see a family therapist immediately. Family therapy will give each member a chance to express his feelings regarding the abuse.
- Plan to set aside regular time for family meetings, a time to hash out problems instead of letting them build up.
- Actively work on learning to communicate effectively with one another. Therapy will help you with this, but if your family does not wish to seek this kind of help, read some books on learning effective communication skills. Some of these skills will be discussed in the last chapter.

4. MAKE A MUTUAL AGREEMENT.

As with all reconciliations, it is necessary for you and other family members to bury the hatchet and go on. This means that you must call a cease-fire and work together toward establishing a healthier relationship. Your agreement might include any of the following mutual commitments:

- We will not continue to fight and verbally abuse each other. We will talk things out, look for solutions, and seek outside help when needed.
- We agree to listen to one another. (This may mean that you must take turns talking while the other listens, making no comments.)
- We agree to stop blaming one another. It is okay to express anger, but we will confine our statements to "I" statements, such as "I feel angry with you, because it sounds as if you don't completely believe what I am telling you," instead of "You still don't believe me—you're calling me a liar."
- We agree to try to explain why we are angry instead of flying off the handle.

You may not be ready for a reconciliation if all you want to do is rage at family members or if this is true of them. If either you or they cannot get past the anger long enough to make some agreements, then the time is simply not right, no matter how much you want it to be. Perhaps more time needs to be spent apart while each of you releases your anger in constructive ways or works on it in therapy.

THE RECONCILIATION PROCESS

If you and your relative(s) decide to begin seeing each other again, make sure you take it slow and easy. You've been out of each other's lives for a while, and it's likely you've both changed in the process. Your family hasn't been the center of your world, and you haven't been the center of theirs. You have new people in your life, new interests. Here are some suggestions on how to ease back into each other's lives:

- See each other less often than you used to
- See each other for shorter periods of time than before
- If you are still somewhat afraid of a family member, try seeing him only when there are others present
- Work on communicating your needs better, such as saying no when you do not want to do something
- Work hard at not slipping into old patterns of letting family members control you or of trying to change family members.

Many survivors are pleased with the results of their attempt at reconciliation. They find that since they have become stronger and more mature they are now able to have a relationship with family members that is far healthier than ever before.

On the other hand, some attempts at reconciliation simply reinforce the survivor's resolve to remain estranged from her family. It is sometimes necessary to try a reconciliation in order to quiet the incessant doubting and internal questioning. Attempts that do not work out should never be seen as failures. After all, you control only your end of any relationship. Although you may want a reconciliation with all your heart, other family members may not be willing or able to reciprocate at this time. If this ends up being your situation, you will have two choices: either wait a while and try again or decide to go on with your life without them. Many survivors have discovered that it is necessary to create a new "family of choice" to replace their "family of origin." Because some families never recover, survivors cannot wait for reconciliation to carry on with their lives.

11

IF A SURVIVOR HAS 'DIVORCED' YOU

For Family Members

So far, this book has been about how to respond to a survivor when she disclosed her abuse so as to encourage communication and family unity. If you are reading this chapter, however, it is because the survivor has already talked to you or attempted to do so and the results were not very positive. Many times survivors feel compelled to separate either temporarily or permanently from a family member who they feel either does not believe them or is not supportive of them regarding the sexual abuse. In addition, many survivors feel so betrayed and damaged by a perpetrator who is a family member that they simply cannot continue a relationship with him. This is especially true if the perpetrator does not admit the abuse or does not agree to enter psychotherapy or a treatment program.

Some adult children are faced with the difficult task of severing all ties with their entire family—not just one member. This decision is based on their belief that the entire family is severely dysfunctional and that the only way for them to be healthy is to break away from the family altogether. They may believe that no one in their family is healthy enough to be around their children. They believe that the abuse, alcoholism, neglect, or overcontrol has damaged their siblings to the point that they are either poor role models for their children or a potential danger to them.

It is not always the adult child who makes the break. Some are cast out of the family because they dared to talk about the sexual abuse or because they reported their parents, grandparents, or siblings to the police or to child protective services in order to prevent them from abusing or continuing to abuse their nieces, cousins, or other children. Exposing the family secrets may have enraged other family members: "How could you report your own father?" "How dare you tell those lies?" "Why couldn't you just keep it within the family where it should be? We watch him, we don't let him do that anymore, why did you have to bring in the police?"

Whether your relative has separated or divorced from one family member or the entire family, whether the break was the survivor's idea or the idea of the rest of the family, it is important to realize that there is still hope for reconciliation in the family. This is especially true if you're willing to take certain steps:

1. To have empathy for your loved one and what she has been through.
2. To swallow your pride and to admit that you acted either too hastily, defensively, or too protectively toward the perpetrator.
3. To listen to her, perhaps in a way that you could not before.
4. To admit that you were abusive to her.

Some people don't understand why a family member has separated from or divorced them. If this is the case with you, it would behoove you to read or reread part I of this book. More than likely though, you probably aren't totally in the dark as to her reasons for this estrangement. Chances are that you have known she was unhappy with you for quite some time. She may have been distant from you for a long time but you neglected to ask her what was wrong. She may have tried to tell you about how you hurt her or about behavior or attitudes of yours that have offended her, but you were unwilling to listen. If you would like to reestablish the relationship with your relative, you must be willing to listen to her now. And if you feel you have already listened, you will need to do so in a different way than you did before.

Recently, I had a call from a very distraught father whose daughter had told him five years ago that her older brother had sexually molested her. At that time, the father didn't believe a word of his daughter's accusations. He chalked it up to sibling rivalry, or as his daughter's attempt to get back at her brother for bullying her when she was a kid.

Five years later, the father was feeling extremely remorseful because he now believed his daughter, but she was no longer having any contact with him. When I asked the father why he now believed her, he told me he had recently discovered that the same son had also sexually molested one of his nephews. After many months of coaxing, his daughter had reluctantly agreed to see him one more time. The father wanted some advice about how to relate to his daughter, because he knew he probably had only one more chance.

If you feel like you may have only one more chance, the information in this chapter will help you make the most of your reconciliation efforts. Before you even attempt a reconciliation, you will need to be willing to:

1. Acknowledge to yourself that you have been wrong for one or more of the following:
   • Sexually abusing her
   • Not protecting her better
   • Not believing her when she told you before
   • Protecting the perpetrator
   • Not backing her up with the family
   • Siding with the perpetrator
   • Continuing to associate with the perpetrator.
2. Ask yourself if you are willing to admit this to your estranged relative.
3. Ask yourself if you have changed enough or are willing to change enough to warrant a reconciliation.

Initiating Reconciliation

The first step toward reconciliation is to open your mind and your heart to your loved one. The fact that you are reading this book indicates that you have already done so to some degree. Perhaps you are more educated now about the issue of child sexual abuse, having heard about it through the media or by reading books such as this one. Perhaps one or more of your friends have even told you about their experiences with child sexual abuse. Perhaps your memories of your own victimization are starting to surface. Or perhaps you believe your loved one now because someone else in the family has confided in you that she, too, was abused by the same person. For whatever reason, if you are now more willing to believe what your loved one was trying to tell you, then this is wonderful news for both the survivor and for you. Even though it is painful, facing the truth does set you free and may help you to get back your child, sibling, grandchild, niece, or nephew.

The next thing you will need to do is to swallow your pride. If a family member has stopped seeing you, you may already have come to the conclusion that you miss and need her more than you need your pride. This is exactly the conclusion that Bill came to:

"When my son accused my father of molesting him, I became irate. Frank had always been a troublemaker, but this time he had gone too far. I knew my father wasn't capable of doing such a thing, and besides, who ever heard of a grandfather molesting one of his grandsons? My father was heterosexual all the way. He didn't have any interest in men, much less little boys. The whole thing was preposterous. I told Frank that unless he recanted his story, I would never see him again, and I meant it. Frank stuck by his story, and I haven't seen him for three years now.

"Recently, though, I have begun to think that perhaps I acted too hastily. I've been hearing so much on television about the sexual abuse of children, and some of the cases have involved men abusing boys. In my day we just never heard of such things, but I guess they were going on, nevertheless. My father died recently, and for some reason this left me wondering whether what Frank told me might not be true. I miss

Frank so much, and I want us to have a better relationship than I had with my father. I just don't know how to go about telling him all this. I don't care about having to admit that I may have been wrong, but I just don't know if Frank will be receptive to me after the way I treated him."

As difficult as it may be for you to be the one to reach out, that is indeed what you will need to do. Your loved one probably feels too afraid, too hurt, and too hopeless to reach out to you. Like Frank, she probably tried for a long time to get you to believe his story or to understand how damaged she was by the abuse, and you were unable or unwilling to do so. She probably came to the conclusion, as many survivors do, that she needed to be away from you in order to recover from the abuse, because your disbelief caused her to doubt herself and her perceptions. And so, she is now probably unable or unwilling to reach out to you, even if she sometimes wants to. She probably believes that it is a lost cause. She doesn't feel it is healthy for her to subject herself to more disappointment or pain from you.

You, then, will have to be the one to initiate reconciliation. And you will need to do so in a way that shows your loved one you are sincere and that you have changed. For instance, you might try *asking* her whether you two can talk, instead of *telling* her you want to talk to her. Or you might admit right away that you were wrong and apologize, if that is what is in order.

You will probably need to be more direct than you are used to being when you call or write. Tell your loved one the purpose of your communication right away—for example, "I have been thinking about what you told me, and I now feel I am more open to believing you. I would like to talk to you further about it." If you feel remorse for not believing her earlier, say so: "I know I was wrong for not believing you before." Most important, state your intentions: "I am willing to listen with an open mind," or "I want to support you now in any way I can."

If you find that as much as you miss your relative, and want to reconcile with her, you nonetheless stubbornly refuse to reach out to her, you may be doing what is called "distancing." Distancing is a defense against pain. It works like this: Someone hurts your feelings; you feel humiliated, devastated. The person who hurt you becomes associated with pain. Some of us are less willing than others to experience our pain. We want to avoid it at all costs, even if it means eliminating from our lives those who have hurt us. Distancing can cause us to write people off, to be in the same room and act as if they are not there, to convince ourselves that we no longer care when in fact we do. Try to work past this resistance by telling yourself the truth—that you really do care about your relative.

Your relative may tell you it is too late—that she has already tried to talk to you to no avail. Whatever the specific issues involved, the bottom line is usually this: most adult children want their parent (or other family member) to admit what he has done to hurt them and to apologize for it.

In order to do this, you must take an honest look at yourself. When you look back on how you have treated your child or relative, do you have any regrets? Can you think of things you may have done, or left undone, that might have hurt her? Chances are that she remembers many of the same incidents and still feels hurt by them.

If your loved one agrees to talk to you again, you will need to be prepared to really listen. You will need to focus all your attention on what she is saying and not think about what you want to say in response. Just listen. Don't interrupt, don't talk back, don't defend yourself, don't argue and don't correct what you think are inaccuracies.

It is difficult to sit quietly and listen to someone tell you about all the bad things you have done, remind you of your shortcomings, or blame you for their unhappiness and their problems. But if you want your child or relative back in your life, this is exactly what you must be willing to do. You must listen with an open mind and an eagerness to learn the truth.

Although what your loved one has to say will undoubtedly be difficult for you to hear, try not to space out or "go away." Take a deep breath, feel your feet on the floor, and refocus your eyes so that you are seeing your loved one clearly. Take a sip of water if you need to. If you still cannot focus on what she is saying, tell her what is happening to you. Tell her that you are having a difficult time hearing her and that it must be because it is too painful. She will undoubtedly understand because she is used to dissociating herself. In fact, that is what she did while she was being abused.

While you are listening to your relative, try to hear exactly what she is saying. Don't jump to conclusions. Don't make assumptions. Just hear the words. For example, you may imagine that she is blaming you for the abuse in some way—blaming you for not knowing it was going on, for not stopping it, or for exposing her to the abuser—when in reality she is doing no such thing. Often when we feel guilty about something, we hear blame from other people when it isn't even there. If you tend to do this, you may become defensive and close down and not be able to truly hear your loved one or to be supportive of her. Whether your loved one blames you for some aspect of the abuse is really irrelevant at this point anyway. What is important is what happened to her, how it made her feel, how it affected her life, and how she feels today. Don't let your own tendency to be self-protective get in the way of truly listening and being supportive.

Later on, after your loved one has finished what she wants to say, if you still believe she was blaming you, then check it out with her. Ask her if in fact she does blame you in any way for the abuse or for not stopping it, and be willing to listen to this, too.

FOR NONOFFENDING PARENTS AND OTHER CARETAKERS

If you are a parent or other caretaker of a survivor, you will need to be prepared for her anger. Many survivors blame their parents for not protecting them better, and this is their right. All children have the right to expect protection from their parents. The anger your loved one feels toward you is normal and to be expected. Again, don't let it prevent you from being there for her. If you can support her now, she will be less inclined to hold on to her anger about your not being there for her in the past.

Your child needs you to put her needs ahead of your own. If you feel guilty about not providing the support and protection she needed as a child, this is your chance to make up for it. Give to her now what you couldn't give to her then. Let her be angry with you if she needs to. Let her blame you. If you are there for her now she will get past the anger and blame. She will recognize that you are giving her what she needs.

If you become defensive, you will only succeed in alienating her further. Instead, examine why you want to deny responsibility. Is it possible that you do feel you could have done something about the abuse? Do you feel you could have been a better parent or that you let your child down in some way? If so, you will be doing yourself as well as your child a great service by telling her about these feelings, apologizing to her, and letting her know that you will do everything within your power to make up for it now.

If you still can't understand why your child has divorced you, perhaps it will help you to review your own past and think about how you were treated as a child. If you were physically, verbally, or sexually abused, neglected, overly controlled, or criticized, the chances are very high that you abused your own children in the same ways. Research shows that those who were abused as children are far more likely to become abusive parents than those who were not abused. Refer to the appendix in the back of the book for a detailed description of the different types of child abuse.

It is not your fault that you were abused, but you are responsible for your own actions as an adult as a consequence of that abuse, as Wanda discovered:

"Looking back on it now, I realize that Tony was constantly badgering and berating Crystal. My brothers had treated me the same way when I was growing up, so you would think that I would feel protective of my daughter, but for some reason I didn't. Instead, I told her to just stay away from him. I realize now that I should have talked to Tony and made him stop. In some ways I guess I gave Tony permission to terrorize his sister by not stopping him, but I felt just as helpless about it as I did when I was a kid with my own brothers. Crystal needed me to protect her, to stand up for her, and I didn't. By the time he started sexually molesting her, I guess she had given up on getting any help from me."

Like Wanda, if you wish to reconcile with your adult child, you will need to acknowledge to her that your behavior was neglectful or abusive. Then you need to apologize and ask her what she needs from you now. She may need only an apology for your having abused or neglected her in the past. An honest apology from an abusive or neglectful parent can be incredibly healing to an adult child. Or it may be that you are still being abusive in some way and need to begin working on your problems, whatever they may be. You may need to join a group such as Parents United (for sexually abusive parents and their partners), Parents Anonymous (for parents who have been physically or emotionally abusive to their children), Alcoholics Anonymous (for alcoholics or alcohol abusers), Al-Anon (for partners and relatives of alcoholics), or CODA (for codependents)—whatever applies to you. A listing of these organizations will be provided in the back of the book. You may also need to seek therapy. It would also be a positive gesture for you to offer to pay for your child's therapy if she tells you that she has required treatment because of your abusive or neglectful behavior toward her.

Even if you are able to apologize for your actions, don't expect your adult child to be willing to reconcile right away. She will probably still need to release anger. Much of this anger can be released in therapy or in ways that don't involve you. However, your child may need to release her anger directly toward you in order to heal from the abuse. As the ultimate act of love and kindness, you might consider allowing your child to vent her anger toward you in person as long as she is not abusive.

Above all, your adult child deserves to have you treat her with respect. This may mean not getting drunk in front of her, not making derogatory remarks to her, or not looking at her seductively. It may mean treating her as an adult instead of a child, and not trying to control her or tell her how to run her life.

Living in the Past

As much as we all don't want to admit it, sometimes we are all selfish. We think of our own needs first, even if we are mothers. If your initial reaction to your child's telling you about the sexual abuse was to deny it, get angry with her, or blame her, it is because you were desperately trying to protect yourself from a pain that you imagine is unbearable. Believing your child will mean that absolutely nothing in your life will ever be the same. Louise was finally able to be honest with herself about her reasons for not believing her daughter: "I didn't want to believe my daughter because I knew that if I did I would have to divorce my husband. I couldn't bear to have him touch me one more time, to sleep in the same bed with him even. Believing my daughter meant that my entire relationship with my husband was a lie."

While it is true that the abuse should never have happened or that it should have been dealt with years ago, the fact is it did happen and it wasn't dealt with. It won't do anyone any good if you chastise yourself for what you should have done. You did what you did for a good reason (most likely because you were abused yourself as a child), and it is time to focus on what you can do now. Forgive yourself for not being equipped to deal with it then. You have a choice: stay with your guilt and grief over how horrendous the situation is, or seize the opportunity to give to your child the support she now needs in order to recover.

It is never too late for a parent to offer support. While your child may be angry with you for any of the reasons we have already discussed, try to hear her anger. Let her know that it makes sense that she is angry. This will go a long way toward healing her wounds and renewing your relationship.

Your first real challenge will be to accept that the sexual abuse did occur. Continuing to disbelieve your child contributes to the family dysfunction and to your family's tendency to deny and repress the truth. To be believed is essential to the survivor's recovery.

What to Do to Take Care of Yourself

The best thing you can do for yourself is to make sure you don't get stuck in blame. Blaming yourself is different from taking responsibility. When we blame ourselves we remain stuck in the past, further damaging our self-esteem. Taking responsibility for our actions or inactions, however, is a positive step toward doing something in the present.

Blaming yourself for what happened to your child is not going to help her now. What is going to help is for you to believe her, to take a stand against the perpetrator, and to back her up in the family. Doing these things isn't going to take away the pain your child feels or make up for what you didn't do when she was a child, but it will help her recover in ways you could never imagine.

In addition, you should not allow your child to continue to blame you indefinitely. Remember that although you are responsible for failing to protect her, you are not responsible for the abuse itself.

You also deserve support and may need to talk to others about your feelings and your difficulties during this process. A few visits to a therapist who is well versed in sexual-abuse issues, support groups for parents of survivors, and workshops on the recovery process can be helpful and make your task much easier.

It is rare for a survivor to reject a sincere attempt on the part of a family member to reconcile, especially when the relative is open to the truth and has made some significant changes. If you find that your loved one is not open to the possibility of a reconciliation at this time, back off for now and try again later. It may be that the survivor needs more time away from the family in order to complete her recovery process. Beginning therapy yourself will help you to cope with the continuing separation. It will also indicate to the survivor that you are serious about changing.

For perpetrators

It certainly is no surprise that many survivors do not wish to continue a relationship with their perpetrator, even if that person is also their father, mother, grandparent, sibling, aunt, or uncle. Even though you are their flesh and blood and an integral part of the family, some survivors simply cannot have a relationship with someone who hurt them so deeply. Sometimes the betrayal of trust cannot be mended.

On the other hand, if your relative has severed all ties with you, you can probably do something about it. Many survivors desperately want to resume a relationship with a relative who abused them, but they must first believe that you have learned from your mistakes.

You are wasting your time and that of the survivor and causing needless pain for the entire family if you initiate reconciliation without being prepared to admit total responsibility for the sexual abuse. In order for reconciliation to be any kind of a possibility, you will need to be willing to do the following:

- Admit that you sexually abused the survivor
- Take complete and utter responsibility for the abuse, including apologizing to the survivor, being willing to go to the family and tell them that you abused the survivor, and attempting to make restitution
- Be willing to listen to the survivor's anger and hurt
- Seek therapy.

Admit that you sexually abused the survivor.

We discussed this step extensively in Part I. Suffice to say that unless you are now able to do this, there is no real possibility of reconciliation with your relative. How can the survivor forgive you for something you are not willing to admit you did? Lawrence came to understand this and to realize what he had to do to get his daughter back:

"I thought I would go to my grave insisting that I never touched my daughter inappropriately. It wasn't that I didn't want to apologize to her. I regretted what I had done every day of my life. But I just wasn't willing to accept the consequences of what might happen once I admitted it. I was afraid my wife would leave me and that I would be humiliated in my community. But finally, the more time went by without seeing my daughter, the more I realized that all that didn't matter as much as my getting her back in my life."

Take responsibility for your actions against the survivor.

Also mentioned in Part I was the fact that in addition to admitting the abuse, you must take complete responsibility for it. This means not blaming anyone else for your actions, including the survivor. In addition, you will need to do the following:

1. Admit to yourself that what you did was wrong, regardless of what led you to do it.
2. Learn from your mistake so that you will not repeat it. Get therapy so that you will not continue molesting other children. Make a commitment to yourself to never hurt someone like that again.
3. Be accountable for your actions in any of the following ways:
   • Apologize to the survivor
   • Admit to the family that you abused your relative
   • Make restitution to this person in the best way possible, offering to pay for the therapy the survivor has already had or will need in order to recover from the damage you have caused her.

Be willing to listen to the survivor's anger and hurt.

Throughout this book I have advised family members about the importance of being willing to listen to the survivor's feelings of anger and hurt. But there is no one the survivor needs to have listen to her more than you. She desperately needs you to listen while she tells you how you hurt, betrayed, frightened, and angered her. While this certainly won't be easy, it will be one of the most beneficial things you can do for the survivor, for yourself, and for the family. Listening to the survivor will help her rid herself of the hatred, guilt, fear, and pain that have plagued her since you first crossed over the line with her. Listening to how you hurt her, damaged her, and robbed her of her self-esteem and innocence will help you to come to terms with what you did. And if your family is to come back together, it will be because the survivor has been listened to, believed, and understood.

Seek therapy.

Unless you enter psychotherapy or a treatment program for sex offenders, you are not really admitting to yourself that you have a problem. Unless you seek professional help, you are endangering any child who will ever be around you. And until you take this important step, the survivor will not believe that you are serious about changing.

Marcus told me about his reluctance to come into therapy: "I was afraid of going into therapy. I didn't want someone analyzing me or poking around in my head. But I knew that the only way to prove to my children that I was serious about changing was to take the plunge. At first I was petrified about talking about myself and my own abuse experience, but soon it proved to be one of the best things that I ever did for myself. I didn't realize how much shame I still had from being sexually abused myself as a child and how I had carried that shame into my adulthood. Through therapy I have come to understand why I abused my daughters and to realize that while I may still have the urge to abuse I can learn to control that urge. Although I went into therapy to save my family, I ended up saving myself."

Unless you do all of the above, the chances of a successful reconciliation with your relative or your entire family are minimal. Not only will you need to live the rest of your life without your relative but you may also miss out on seeing your grandchildren or nieces and nephews grow up. Your pride, your good name in the community, even your marriage is not worth that. You, more than anyone else in the family, have the potential to totally turn your family around. While the going will certainly be tough for a while, you will eventually be rewarded with understanding, support, forgiveness, and closeness if you can work past your fears and do what your heart tells you is right.

Bringing your family back together will take the effort of all its members. It will take time, patience, and perseverance, but the rewards will be enormous. In the concluding chapter, I will discuss more ways of communicating effectively with one another. I will also explain how to break the negative patterns that led to the abuse, dysfunction, and secretiveness in your family.

12

WORKING TOGETHER FOR A HEALTHY FAMILY

Recovery from childhood sexual abuse takes immense courage, patience, and perseverance on the survivor's part and on the part of her family of origin. There are no quick solutions. The process sometimes seems endless, the pain sometimes overwhelming, but it is worth all the time, pain, and hard work. Each member of the family will be rewarded with freedom from the pain of the past, and the entire family will be rewarded with better communication and closer, healthier relationships. Nothing can erase the abuse from your lives. But with the secret out in the open, you will find that your family functions in a far more loving, healthy, and honest way and that relationships that have been strained, damaged or even severed can be mended and renewed.

The next step will be to bring your family together with the express purpose of improving your communication and breaking some of the unhealthy patterns and ways of relating that have been contributing factors in allowing the sexual abuse to take place.

IMPROVING COMMUNICATION WITHIN THE FAMILY

Open and honest communication does not come easily to most people. But because communication is a skill, you can learn it, practice it, and improve on it throughout your life. Following these basic rules will help you improve your communication skills:

1. INITIATE OPEN COMMUNICATION.

Don't always wait for someone else in the family to bring up a sensitive issue. Take the initiative. The more openly and honestly you share, the more open and honest will be the feedback you get.

2. THINK BEFORE YOU SPEAK.

For the most part, you probably need to work on saying what you feel when you feel it, but try not to use your feelings as carte blanche to attack someone else. Don't just dump all your feelings on the other person. If you phrase your words carefully and thoughtfully, your listener is more likely to hear what you are saying. Consider how the other person will respond to your words. Since words sometimes come out the wrong way in the heat of the moment, use your internal "editor"—the inner voice that questions the appropriateness and timeliness of your comments.

3. MAKE "I" INSTEAD OF "YOU" STATEMENTS.

No one likes to be talked down to, told what to do, or lectured to. Instead of starting your sentences with "You" as in, "You drink too much," or "You are afraid to hear what I have to say," try using "I" messages to convey your feelings, as in "It hurts me to see you drinking so much. I'm afraid you're going to die early or get killed in a car accident," or "I feel like you're avoiding me. I'd like to talk to you."

If another family member does or says something that hurts you, try to say, "I felt hurt when you..." instead of "You stink because you...." Since "I" statements are less blaming, they allow you to say what you feel when you feel it, without making the other person feel overly defensive.

4. LEARN HOW TO LISTEN.

Members of dysfunctional families often do not listen to one another closely enough to understand what the speaker is saying. They may not really want to hear what the other family member is saying, assume they know what the other person is going to say, or have their mind on other things.

In learning to really listen to other family members you must focus your attention completely onto the person who is speaking. You must avoid thinking about what *you* want to say. Put your own agenda aside as you are listening.

Make eye contact with the other person for as long as it is comfortable. Position your body in a way that communicates openness and receptiveness (uncross your arms, sit up straight). As you are listening, give small nods to show that you are paying attention.

Learn active listening. In order to listen actively, you will need to paraphrase, or restate, what the other family member is saying from time to time. This will let the other person know you are really listening. It will also keep your mind on the conversation instead of other things. And it will clear up any misunderstandings right on the spot.

When you paraphrase, you find out if the message you received was in fact the message the speaker intended to send. This helps to keep the communication clear and understood. You can paraphrase either content or feelings. When you paraphrase content you restate the main idea as you have heard it:

> **SPEAKER:** "We never get together as a family anymore. No one even knows what the others are doing."
>
> **LISTENER:** "You want us to be more of a family."

If you are accurate in your paraphrasing, the speaker will tell you so. If you aren't, she will correct your interpretation. In either case, you've accomplished what you set out to do, which is to clarify the message.

When you paraphrase feelings, you tell the other person what you imagine she is feeling based on what she has been telling you:

SPEAKER: "I really wish you wouldn't have pornographic magazines around the house for my kids to see."
LISTENER: "You're afraid your kids will get hold of them."

5. ONLY ONE PERSON TALKS AT A TIME.

This may sound like a ridiculous rule, because we all know that only one person can talk at a time and be heard, but it is amazing how many families do not follow this simple and obvious rule. Two, three, sometimes four people will be trying to speak at the same time, all trying to get their point across simultaneously. But when there are so many people talking, who is listening? Probably no one. Everyone is so concerned about being heard that no one is listening to anyone else. Try to establish a new rule: When someone is speaking, everyone else listens.

6. AVOID SAYING "ALWAYS" AND "NEVER."

Not only are these absolute generalizations usually not true, they also indicate that you have lost perspective. If you tell someone he never listens to you, it will make him angry and leave him feeling like there is no way he can ever please you. A better way of handling the situation might be to seek the other person's help: "When you continue to do what I asked you not to do, it makes me feel like you are not listening to me or that you don't care about my feelings." This should elicit an apology or at least an explanation.

If someone in the family uses such absolute phrasing on you, try to see his point. Say something like "It may seem that way to you, and I know that what you're saying may have been true in the past. But let's talk about it. Is that the real issue, or are you upset about something else?"

7. DON'T ARGUE OR ATTEMPT TO CHANGE SOMEONE ELSE'S MIND.

If you don't feel understood, repeat what you were just saying in a different way and then ask the person to paraphrase what you said.

8. GIVE EACH OTHER TIME TO THINK ABOUT WHAT HAS BEEN SAID.

Don't insist on an immediate response to something you have just shared. Typically, we tend to be more defensive in the moment, more invested in being right.

9. RESPECT THE OTHER PERSON'S WISH TO DISENGAGE FROM A CONVERSATION.

You can't force people to communicate against their will. It may seem like the perfect time for you to get into a heavy discussion with another family member, but he may feel it's the wrong time. Accept and respect this feeling. If you believe this discussion is so important that it's essential to the relationship, then try to schedule a future date when you will both feel comfortable discussing it.

10. NO COMMENT.

You don't always have to comment on what the other person says if you disagree with it. Feel free to say nothing or to say "I hear what you're saying" or "I'm sorry you feel that way." Obviously, this doesn't mean you should sit in stony silence or withdraw in hostility because you don't like or agree with what the other person is saying. But if you feel you can react only with anger, you may be better off postponing any response.

11. SET STRICT LIMITS ON PERMISSIBLE COMMUNICATION.

When words or actions become abusive, communication no longer has any meaning. No one has the license to be verbally or physically abusive to you in "trying to make a point." Remember always to give yourself permission to remove yourself from any interchange that you consider unhealthy, unproductive, or abusive. In withdrawing, simply say something like "I find your remarks insulting and your behavior unacceptable. I can't listen to this anymore. I need to take care of myself." Don't allow communication to go beyond the limit of mutual respect.

Mastering these communication skills will simultaneously help you to hear and to be heard by other family members. As your communication skills develop, you will find it easier to become more honest and open.

BREAKING DYSFUNCTIONAL PATTERNS OF RELATING

In Part II I introduced you to the eight types of interactions found in all abusive families: denial, inconsistency and unpredictability, lack of empathy, lack of clear boundaries, role reversal, the closed family system, incongruent communication, and extremes in conflict. It is vitally important that each individual in the family and the family as a whole work on changing these negative patterns. Please refer now to Chapter 8, section II to remind yourself of the definitions of these dysfunctional elements.

COUNTERACTING DENIAL

When one person breaks through the web of denial in a repressed family, as the survivor does in the case of disclosure, the other members often resent that change. They may try anything to restore the old family pattern, from gently cajoling the survivor back into the familiar role to threatening her with angry, critical, and condemning statements.

In addition, sexual abuse is rarely the only problem in a family. Therefore, when a survivor discloses to her family that she was sexually abused, other issues and family problems are likely to emerge. Other "secret" events, hidden relationships, and unexpressed feelings that have been carefully guarded are suddenly brought out in the open.

One survivor recalled the following experience: "It wasn't until I told my mother that I had been sexually abused by my father that I found out he was not my real father after all but my stepfather. I think I was about as shocked to learn this as my mother was to learn he had abused me. Since then, nothing in our family has been the same. I feel betrayed by my stepfather for being sexual with me and by my mother and stepfather for making me believe all this time that he was my real father."

Another said: "When I told my mother I had been sexually abused by my uncle, she told me that he was a homosexual."

And a third remembered: "When I told my brother I had been sexually abused by our grandfather, my brother confronted me with the fact that I had sexually abused *him* when we were kids."

Keeping secrets is probably one of the most negative processes that can occur in a family. It is not just the secret itself that is important but the process in which the family engages to maintain the secret. Secrets divide family members. Secret-keeping is based on collusion and exclusion. Although excluded family members are often, in fact, aware of the secret, they feel unable to address the issues the secret represents symbolically. Secret-keeping is a dysfunctional family process that makes certain family members feel special and connected while excluding other family members who are seen as being vulnerable, responsible, and/or outside important family matters.

In addition, since family myths are being exploded, everyone may suddenly begin to unleash anger, old resentments, judgments and criticisms that have been suppressed for years for the sake of presenting a picture of family togetherness to the outside world.

Now that the secrets are out, it is time to regroup, to express the feelings you haven't shared, to react to all the new information and to deal with the issues that have been exposed.

Stop denying or minimizing the truth. Stop pretending that things are better than they are. Acknowledge that things are bad, that your family is dysfunctional, that there are serious problems in your family. Let the secrets out.

CREATING CONSISTENCY AND PREDICTABILITY

Sit down together as a family and decide on some basic family rules. These rules should represent the needs of each individual in the family as well as the family as a group. For example, "No drunkenness around the children," "No talking behind each other's back," and "No telling of dirty jokes around other family members" might be some good rules for your family to consider.

Instead of family rules, you may want to talk about what is most important in the family and make some agreements as to how you as a family can go about achieving these goals. For example, if what is most important is that the children in the family are protected (as it should be), you may agree as a family that the perpetrator will never be left alone with the children, that the perpetrator will seek therapy, and that you will all be supportive of the perpetrator as he recovers.

Or, if the family agrees that what is important is that you continue to talk about problems as they build up, then agree to have family meetings once a month and to permit any family member to call a meeting whenever he feels it is necessary.

The important thing is that you provide some consistency and predictability in the family to replace the chaos and instability that has defined it in the past.

GAINING EMPATHY

Empathy is the ability to put yourself in another person's shoes and imagine what she is feeling. Often members of dysfunctional families are unable to do this and this adds to the distance and misunderstanding between them.

It is important that you learn not just to listen to one another but to listen *empathetically*. As you listen to another family member, imagine yourself in her situation. What do you think she is feeling?

LEARNING TO SET BOUNDARIES

Begin to develop *discernible* (recognizable as distinct) boundaries between yourself and other members of your family. The dysfunctional family can be likened to a large, sticky mass. Everyone in the family is emotionally "stuck" to everyone else. There is no psychological or emotional separation between one individual and another. Individual identities are lost. Members cling to each other for a sense of security and well-being. This situation of enmeshment is often experienced by the incestuous family as "closeness." Enmeshment, in reality, is a jail sentence locking individuals into a life of false masks, pretense, and an inability to reach personal potential in relationships.

Begin to respect each family member's right to personal space and privacy. Knock before entering the bathroom or a family member's bedroom and lock the bathroom door when you enter. Only read mail that is addressed to you personally, and do not read other family members' diaries or journals. Teach your children to do the same. Do not allow your children to sleep with or take showers with you or with any other family member. Do not walk around the house naked, and ask other family members to respect your wishes and discontinue this practice around your children. Do not watch your children while they take baths and use the toilet or allow any other adult in the family to do so. Do not allow older brothers to sleep with younger sisters. Teach your children to say no to anyone who tries to touch them when they do not want to be touched. This includes saying no to relatives who want to kiss them or hold them in their lap. Teach your children that they have rights, too.

Since your family has psychological and physical boundaries that are enmeshed and confused you will need to establish your own boundaries more clearly. And realize that family enmeshment can be mistaken for true need fulfillment or love. Its dissolution can feel like a tremendous loss.

REVERSING ROLE REVERSAL

If you grew up in a family where you were expected to take care of your parents' needs, you will have a tendency to treat your own children in the same way. Make certain that you break the cycle by not turning to your children to meet your needs for support, advice, affection, or sex. Allow your children to be children instead of expecting them to be little adults (running a household, taking care of younger siblings, earning money for the family).

In addition, you may need to reverse the role reversal that may still exist between you and your parent(s). While it is no longer your parents' responsibility to take care of your needs or to protect you, neither is it *your* responsibility to meet their needs. For example, it is not your job to take care of your mother, even if your father does beat her up, or to pick your father up at the bar because he can't drive, or to undress him and put him to bed.

OPENING UP THE FAMILY

Begin to counter the isolation you probably experienced growing up and which may still exist within your family by establishing friendships outside the family, and encourage your children to do the same. Do not depend only on family members to be your support. Reach out to others for solace and guidance.

COMMUNICATING CLEARLY

Work at communicating clearly instead of giving mixed messages. Say what you mean and mean what you say. Counter the incongruent messages you received as a child by being very clear and consistent with your own children. When other family members give you mixed messages, ask them to clarify what they mean.

RESOLVING CONFLICTS

As you improve your communication skills, your family will need to learn how to settle conflicts peacefully and to everyone's satisfaction. This will be one of your biggest challenges. Although everyone has some conflict in his or her family, not all people express their conflicting feelings. While some people let the fur fly, others silently seethe, refusing even to acknowledge conflict. When people avoid conflict, the tension between them builds.

You can't simply wish conflicts away. Most people react to conflict by thinking, "If only you loved me, you'd agree with me." This kind of immature and wishful thinking tends to escalate conflict instead of resolving it. This attitude denies another person's right to differ from you, essentially sending the message, "If you really love me, you have to think, feel, and be exactly like me." It places all responsibility for resolving disagreements—and all power to change—in the hands of the other person.

The first step toward resolving conflict involves acknowledging its existence. It may be easier for you to admit to disagreements if you recognize that conflict is essential to your growth and the growth of the family. In fact, every relationship inevitably involves a clash of needs, opinions, and feelings.

The next step is to recognize that, contrary to what you may have learned growing up, not all differences are irreconcilable, and not all conflicts are unresolvable. In fact, most conflicts can be resolved amicably if both people are willing to communicate and work toward that end. If you keep these things in mind, you won't need to be afraid to disagree with another family member.

The next step will be for the entire family to agree to work out your disagreements together. Thus, when conflicts arise, you need to approach resolution with the goal of coming closer together. If those in conflict stubbornly try to force the other person to change or to prove that one is right and the other is wrong, reconciliation becomes impossible. You will all need to let go of the kind of black-and-white thinking that sees only right or wrong possibilities in arguments.

There is much to be gained by going through the process of recovery together as a family. With a lot of hard work and the personal investment of each family member, you can eventually enjoy a family environment where there are no more secrets, where the family can enlarge itself to include outside intimate friends, where personal privacy is respected, where freedom to come and go is encouraged, where conflicts are expressed and resolved. In spite of their good intentions and their hard work, however, many families find that they just can't do it on their own. The following section will answer some of your questions about individual and family therapy and help you find the right therapist.

FINDING THE RIGHT TYPE OF THERAPY AND THE RIGHT THERAPIST

Each person in the family needs professional help in order to recover from the damage caused by childhood sexual abuse. Some members of the family—the survivor and the perpetrator, most notably—will need long-term individual psychotherapy in addition to any therapy the family becomes involved in. Siblings and sometimes the nonoffending parent may be able to get the help they need in the context of family therapy.

THERAPY FOR SURVIVORS

Survivors need to be in individual therapy with a professional who specializes in helping victims of childhood sexual abuse. Individual therapy will provide them with the opportunity to develop trusting, honest, healthy relationships—perhaps for the first time.

In addition to entering individual therapy, many survivors find help in recovery groups, which offer them the chance to discover that there are others who share their feelings. Such groups provide a safe place for the exploration of feelings that will surface as an inevitable part of the healing process. They also offer valuable support, feedback, and accurate information about such subjects as the effects of child abuse on sexuality, and ways of breaking through problems with intimacy.

ENCOURAGING A MALE SURVIVOR TO SEEK HELP

Because there has been so little information regarding the sexual abuse of male children, most men have felt that they must suffer alone. Believing that few other men shared their situation, they have felt isolated and freaky. Generally speaking, men are particularly reluctant to seek therapy, and even those who do are often unable to tell their therapist they were sexually abused for fear of being judged. Many men have difficulties reaching out for help because they feel they need to appear tough and macho. But although they may not let others see their suffering it remains just under the surface.

Some men have attempted to reach out only to have their worst fears come true. They were indeed discounted, blamed, or treated insensitively. While it will be particularly difficult for them to reach out for help again, it is important to understand that times have changed. There is now a far greater understanding of males who were sexually abused as children than ever before. Many therapists have had special training in this field and understand the special problems of the male sex-abuse victim.

When a male survivor repeats the cycle of abuse by molesting children, he will be particularly reluctant to seek help for fear of being judged, criticized, or even reported to the police. But if he can come to understand that he is a victim of his own childhood abuse and is no more in control of himself than an alcoholic, he may be able to see therapy for exactly what it is—the only way out of a vicious cycle, a cycle that hurts himself as well as others.

Tell the male survivor in your family that help is available. Men all over the country are now recovering from the damage caused by sexual abuse. Hundreds of recovery groups now exist, and many therapists are trained to handle the special needs of male sex-abuse victims. It takes courage to reach out for help, but if your relative can find the courage, he will discover that there is indeed hope.

TREATMENT FOR THE PERPETRATOR

Expertise in working with offenders is improving, although many communities still lack the proper resources. It is not true that effective treatment can occur only with offenders who are motivated to get help, even though this attitude is widespread. Programs have successfully treated offenders who were pressured into therapy through threats of prison or parole revocation.

Most incestuous abusers require more than family therapy to keep them from abusing again. Some of the most serious issues behind incestuous abuse, such as a history of childhood trauma, may not be adequately dealt with in family therapy. Therefore individual therapy is also necessary.

While therapists disagree on the effectiveness of some treatment methods, many techniques for dealing with child sex offenders have proven successful. The real issue is not whether an effective approach exists, but rather how to match approaches to types of offenders.

The treatment of child sex offenders is a highly specialized field, and most clinicians, including many who treat other types of offenders, are not skilled enough to treat them. For this reason you will need to be especially diligent in finding someone who has the expertise that you will need in order to recover from your problems.

FAMILY THERAPY

In family therapy, the entire family is seen by a therapist or sometimes two therapists working as a team. The therapist's focus should be on the entire family and how it interacts, never on only one or two members. For this reason, the family should not be treated by a therapist who has already seen one member of the family for more than one session.

Ideally, the entire family should begin therapy together. Depending upon the therapist's theoretical orientation, he or she may decide after the first session to have one individual session with each family member; thereafter, the family will be seen as a unit.

The family therapy session should be safe for all members. The therapist should exhibit and encourage respect for individual differences within the family. Family members are worried that they will be scapegoated, held responsible for the problem, focused on excessively, invalidated, and so forth. It is a great relief to family members to leave the first session feeling respected and understood and to have had the opportunity to explain their view of the problems to the rest of the family.

In the initial phase of therapy, some family members may choose to be silent. Some may tell their concerns through stories and humor. Others may choose to be angry for a while. A good therapist will understand that the various types of behavior exhibited by family members early in therapy represent their ways of coping. When they realize that the family therapist is not going to judge them, control them, and/or evaluate them, they will begin to relax and involve themselves in a positive way in the process.

SELECTING A THERAPIST

One of the best ways of finding a competent individual or family therapist is to get a referral from someone you know—a friend who has had similar problems or your medical doctor, for example. If you can't get a referral this way, call your local hospital, rape crisis center, or hotline, and ask to be referred to someone who specializes in working with survivors of childhood sexual abuse and their families. It is very important that you go to a therapist who specializes in childhood sexual abuse, because this particular problem requires special training and experience. A referral doesn't mean that this will be the best therapist for you, but it usually indicates that the therapist is respected and known in the community.

INTERVIEWING POTENTIAL THERAPISTS

Choose your therapist carefully. Take into consideration **her** (or his) experience and training, her theoretical orientation regarding sexual abuse; how she treats you; and, most important, *how you feel about her.* In addition, a good therapist needs to be able to convey **warmth, genuine-ness,** and empathy.

The only way you are going to find out this information is to ask questions and to pay attention to how you feel in this person's presence. Answers to these relevant questions will be helpful:

1. What are her qualifications, training, and experience?
2. Does she have experience and training working with the specific problems of childhood sexual abuse? In addition, ask about **her** treatment philosophy and approach with this type of client or problem.
3. Does she seem to be really hearing what you are saying? A good therapist is able to reflect back to you your feelings with reasonable accuracy.
4. Do you feel safe with her? While you will probably be nervous during the first few sessions and may not be comfortable with the questions the therapist is asking, you should feel relatively safe in spite of your discomfort.
5. Does she seem to respect your feelings, opinions, and needs? You should not feel that your experience is being minimized, judged, or criticized.
6. Does she convey genuine caring? You should get the sense that the therapist really cares but is not a rescuer.
7. Is the therapist clear about her own boundaries? The therapist should be there to take care of your needs, not hers. This means that you should never have to listen to a therapist's problems or to feel like you must take care of her feelings. In addition, it means that a therapist should never attempt to be sexually intimate with you.

It is important to have the right "fit" between client and therapist. If the therapist doesn't seem to like you or seems indifferent, you may need to keep looking. You should start the therapy process with a certain amount of warmth and connectedness between you and the therapist.

SUPPORT GROUPS

In addition to therapy, you may want to join a support group that is led by a licensed therapist or affiliated with a 12-step program or an organization such as Parents United. Group therapy can be one of the most powerful tools to break down your sense of isolation. Such groups and organizations are listed in Appendix II.

If you have read this book, followed the suggestions I have made, and attempted to work with your family to solve your problems, you are a rare individual indeed. Most relatives of survivors are unable to get past their defensiveness regarding the sexual abuse and are therefore unable to focus on the issues that need to be addressed both individually and in the family. Most prefer to keep the family secrets hidden and to avoid the pain of coming out of denial concerning their own abuse. And most prefer to hide in the relative comfort of the enmeshed family rather than to venture outside and risk discovering that there is a healthier way of living.

It is extremely difficult to face the truth about your family, the perpetrator, and even yourself. It would have been easier to protect the family system at the price of the survivor's and your own recovery. It would have been simpler just to call the survivor a liar or a lunatic and to keep your blinders on. But you chose instead to open yourself and your family to honest scrutiny. You chose to feel the pain rather than to live in the void of ignorance. You chose family unity and family health over family enmeshment. And, most important, you chose the growth and integrity that comes from struggling with the truth, facing your most painful emotions, and then coming out the other side.

To inquire about scheduling Beverly Engel for speaking engagements, you may write to her at the address below. She welcomes your feedback and ideas regarding *Families in Recovery* but regrets that because of the volume of requests, she is unable to answer individual letters and phone calls. (Please refer to the organizations in Appendix II for referrals.)

Beverly Engel
P.O. Box 552
Cambria, CA 93428

APPENDIX I

Some Essential Terms and Information about Childhood Sexual Abuse

The following are the words most commonly used when discussing childhood sexual abuse. You may have heard them often and yet not know exactly what they mean:

Child Sexual Abuse—Any action that is intended to sexually stimulate the perpetrator or the victim, where the victim is a child and the perpetrator is an adult or an older child.

Child molestation—Used interchangeably with *sexual abuse*.

Incest—The most common form of child sexual abuse, incest is any sexual contact between a child or adolescent and a person who is closely related or perceived to be related, such as a parent, sibling, cousin, uncle or aunt, grandparent, stepparents, and live-in partners of parents. Sometimes the definition of incest is extended to include sexual abuse by any person in a position of authority or responsibility over the child.

SURVIVOR—Anyone who has survived an abusive or neglectful childhood. The word implies that the person no longer has to be a victim.

PROSURVIVOR—Anyone who is a caring supporter of a survivor (e.g., a mate, lover, friend, family member, counselor).

PERPETRATOR—The sexual abuser or molester. Experts in the sexual-abuse field have adopted this word from police officers to emphasize that childhood sexual abuse is indeed a crime.

ABUSER—Some people prefer this word instead of perpetrator because it can be more descriptive and clear.

OFFENDER—Used interchangeably with perpetrator and abuser.

SILENT PARTNER—Anyone who knew or should have known that the sexual abuse was occurring. In other words, anyone who made it possible for the perpetrator to abuse the child, by not protecting, supervising, or nurturing the child properly. The term is commonly used in cases of father/daughter or mother/son incest to refer to the nonoffending parent. It implies that both husband and wife were actually in a partnership, no matter how unconscious. Some psychologists insist that the silent partner is a participant whether she knows about the incest or not, though her participation is often characterized more by what she does not do than by what she does.

In addition to the terms listed above, there is some general information concerning this issue that will be helpful for you to know. I have presented it in the form of the most-often-asked questions about the subject.

WHAT SPECIFICALLY IS MEANT BY CHILD ABUSE IN GENERAL?

There are basically four categories of child abuse:
1. Physical abuse and corporal punishment or willful cruelty.
2. Physical neglect, inadequate supervision, abandonment.
3. Emotional abuse and deprivation.
4. Sexual molestation, abuse, and sexual exploitation.

1. PHYSICAL ABUSE

Any nonaccidental injury, including violent assault with an implement such as a belt, strap, switch, cord, brush, or paddle, resulting in bruises, welts, burns, broken bones, fractures, scars, or internal injuries. "Spanking" for purely disciplinary reasons is not generally regarded as child abuse, although if bruises result or if a tool is used, it may be judged to be child abuse. Physical abuse also includes being punched, slapped, pulled on, yanked on, choked, shaken, kicked, pinched, or tortured with tickling. It also includes the witnessing of violence done to a parent or sibling.

2. PHYSICAL NEGLECT

Includes abandonment; refusal to seek, allow, or provide treatment for illness or impairment; inadequate physical supervision; disregard of health hazards in the home; failure to provide adequate nutrition, clothing, or hygiene when services are available; keeping a child home from school repeatedly without cause; or failing to enroll a child in school.

3. EMOTIONAL ABUSE

Includes emotional or verbal assaults, such as persistent teasing, belittling, or verbal attacks; close confinement, such as tying a child up or locking him in a closet; inadequate nurturing, such as that affecting failure-to-thrive babies; putting unreasonable demands on a child that are beyond her capabilities, knowingly permitting antisocial behavior, such as delinquency; or ignoring a diagnosed emotional problem.

4. SEXUAL ABUSE

Includes sexual molestation, incest, or exploitation for prostitution, the production of pornographic materials, or any other exploitation of a child for the sexual gratification of an adult. This can include physical sexual abuse, indirect sexual abuse, verbal sexual abuse, boundary violation, and emotional sexual abuse.

- *Physical sexual abuse*: Includes sexualized hugging or kissing, sexual fondling, oral or anal sex, intercourse, masturbation of the victim, or forcing of the victim to masturbate the offender.

- *Indirect sexual abuse*: Includes any act of voyeurism or

exhibitionism on the part of an adult toward a child for the conscious or unconscious sexual stimulation of the adult. With voyeurism, the adult becomes sexually stimulated by watching a child dress, undress, take a bath or shower, or use the toilet.

- *Exhibitionism*: The adult exposes his genitals to the child or walks around naked for the purpose of being sexually stimulated.

- *Verbal sexual abuse*: Includes using inappropriate sexual words or obscenities in an abusive way toward a child, asking inappropriate questions about the child's sexual life or sexual anatomy, talking about sex in front of a child whose age level is inappropriate, or making remarks about the sexual parts of the child's body (for example, remarks about the size of the child's breasts or penis).

- *Boundary violation*: Includes exposure of children to their parents' sexual behavior or naked bodies. It also includes the denying of privacy to a child such as walking in on the child in the bathroom or in his or her bedroom.

- *Emotional sexual abuse*: The inappropriate bonding of one or both parents with one of their children. When a parent uses a child to meet his or her emotional needs, the relationship can easily become sexualized and romanticized. Emotional sexual abuse has also been defined as a parent having a relationship with his child that is more important than the relationship the parent has with his spouse.

213

WHAT EXACTLY IS CHILDHOOD SEXUAL ABUSE?

Many forms of sexual abuse do not involve intercourse or any kind of penetration. Below is an abbreviated version of a list that originally appeared in *Handbook of Clinical Intervention in Child Sexual Abuse* by Suzanne M. Sgroi. The list contains many of the types of sexual abuse toward children of either sex:

NUDITY. The adult parades around the house unclothed in front of all or some of the family members.

DISROBING. The adult disrobes in front of the child, generally when the child and the adult are alone.

GENITAL EXPOSURE. The adult exposes his or her genitals to the child.

OBSERVATION OF THE CHILD. The adult surreptitiously or overtly watches the child undress, bathe, excrete, or urinate.

KISSING. The adult kisses the child in a lingering or intimate way.

FONDLING. The adult fondles the child's breasts, abdomen, genital area, inner thighs, or buttocks. The child may similarly fondle the adult at his or her request.

MASTURBATION. The adult masturbates while the child observes; the adult observes the child masturbating; the adult and child masturbate each other (mutual masturbation).

FELLATIO. The adult has the child fellate him or her, or the adult fellates the child.

CUNNILINGUS. The child places mouth and tongue on the vulva or in the vaginal area of an adult female, or the adult places his or her mouth on the vulva or in the vaginal area of the female child.

DIGITAL (FINGER) PENETRATION OF THE ANUS OR RECTAL OPENING. Perpetrators may also thrust inanimate objects, such as crayons or pencils inside the child's anus.

PENILE PENETRATION OF THE ANUS OR RECTAL OPENING.

DIGITAL (FINGER) PENETRATION OF THE VAGINA. Inanimate objects may also be inserted.

DRY INTERCOURSE. The adult rubs his penis against the child's genital-rectal area or inner thighs or buttocks.

PENILE PENETRATION OF THE VAGINA.

If any of the above-listed acts took place in infancy, childhood, or adolescence with someone older and the child felt uncomfortable or strange about it, then she was sexually abused. Of equal importance is any indirect or direct sexual suggestion made by an adult toward a child. This is called *approach behavior*. It can include sexual looks, innuendo, or suggestive gestures. Even if the adult never engaged in touching or took any overt sexual action, the child picks up these projected sexual feelings.

Keep in mind that the *intention* of the adult or older

child while engaging in some of the acts (nudity, disrobing, observation of the child) will determine whether the act is actually sexually abusive. If an adult watches a child bathe, for example, but does so in a *nonsexual* way that does not upset the child, it may not be sexually abusive. But if the adult becomes sexually aroused while watching, it is then sexual abuse.

DO ALL TYPES OF SEXUAL ABUSE CAUSE DAMAGE? ARE SOME FORMS OF SEXUAL ABUSE MORE DAMAGING THAN OTHERS?

While the list above seems to increase in severity, all types of sexual abuse, even nudity and inappropriate kissing, can damage a child for a lifetime, whether or not the abuse is overly physical or repeated. All types of abuse cause emotional and psychological damage and pain. Much of this damage is caused by the betrayal of someone the child trusted and cared about. Children need time to be children before they are capable of handling any sexual relationship. Sexuality foisted upon them too early amounts to abuse, and it is still abuse even in the complete absence of physical pain.

There are many long-term effects of childhood sexual abuse. Not every person who is sexually abused as a child suffers from each specific problem listed under the broad categories, but most suffer from all the symptoms listed as broad categories.

1. DAMAGE TO SELF-ESTEEM AND SELF-IMAGE

Feeling ugly inside; feelings of worthlessness; a tendency to overapologize; feeling that they are stupid, a failure, a loser; tremendous guilt feelings and feelings of shame; a tendency to blame themselves for whatever goes wrong; a tendency to sabotage success; a tendency to be victimized by others; feelings of helplessness.

2. RELATIONSHIP PROBLEMS

Difficulty trusting others; a tendency to be distant and aloof; a tendency to get involved with destructive people who abuse them physically, emotionally, or sexually; a lack of empathy or concern for others; a deep sense of isolation; difficulty with physical affection; secrecy, evasiveness, and a tendency to withhold information from others or the opposite, a tendency to "tell all"; a tendency to "give themselves away," helping others to the point of not taking care of themselves; difficulties with authority figures; difficulties communicating desires, thoughts, and feelings to others; difficulty receiving from others.

3. SEXUAL PROBLEMS

Lack of sexual desire; inability to enjoy sex or to have an orgasm; sexual dysfunction; inability to enjoy certain types of sexuality; problems with sexual identity; promiscuity; attraction to "illicit" sexual activities such as pornography and prostitution; anger and disgust at any public (or media) display of affection, sexuality, nudity, or partial nudity; a tendency to be sexually manipulative; sexual addiction.

4. EMOTIONAL PROBLEMS

Intense anger and rage that sometimes bursts out unexpectedly; mood swings ranging from deep depression to extreme anxiety; chronic depression; dissociation or a "splitting off" from oneself, including time blockages and feeling of numbness in various parts of their body; extreme fears or phobias; sleep disturbances; addiction to food, alcohol, or drugs; obsessive/compulsive behavior such as compulsive shopping, shoplifting, gambling or cleaning; eating disorders; flashbacks that are triggered by certain sights, sounds, smells, or touches; abusive behavior; self-destructive behavior such as suicide attempts and self-mutilation.

5. PHYSICAL PROBLEMS

Frequent sore throats, difficulty swallowing, migraine headaches, unexplained vaginal or anal pain, frequent bladder and vaginal infections, skin disorders, numbness or tingling in legs or arms.

RECOMMENDED READING

CHILDHOOD SEXUAL ABUSE

Armstrong, I. *Kiss Daddy Goodnight*. New York: Hawthorn, 1978.

Angelou, Maya. *I Know Why the Caged Bird Sings*. New York: Bantam, 1980.

Bass, Ellen, and Laura Davis. *The Courage to Heal: A Guide for Women Survivors of Child Sexual Abuse*. New York: Harper & Row, 1988.

Bass, Ellen and Louise Thornton, eds. *Writings by Women Survivors of Childhood Sexual Abuse*. New York: Harper & Row, 1983.

Brady, Katherine. *Father's Days: A True Story of Incest*. New York: Dell, 1979.

Butler, Sandra. *Conspiracy of Silence: The Trauma of Incest*. San Francisco: Volcano Press, 1985 (updated).

Crewdson, John. *By Silence Betrayed: Sexual Abuse of Children in America*. Boston: Little, Brown, 1988.

Engel, Beverly. *The Right to Innocence: Healing the Trauma of Childhood Sexual Abuse*. Fawcett: New York, 1990.

Evert, Kathy. *When You're Ready: A Woman's Healing from Childhood Physical and Sexual Abuse By Her Mother.* Walnut Creek, Calif.: Launch Press, 1987.

Finkelhor, David. *Child Sexual Abuse: New Theory and Research.* New York: The Free Press, 1984.

Forward, Susan and Craig Buck. *Betrayal of Innocence: Incest and Its Devastation.* Los Angeles: Jeremy P. Tarcher, Inc., 1978.

Herman, Judith. *Father–Daughter Incest.* Cambridge: Harvard University Press, 1981.

Lew, Mike. *Victims No Longer: Men Recovering From Incest and Other Sexual Child Abuse.* New York: Harper Collins, 1990.

Love, Patricia. *The Emotional Incest Syndrome: What to do When a Parent's Love Rules Your Life.* New York: Bantam Books, 1990.

Maltz, Wendy, and Beverly Holman. *Incest and Sexuality: A Guide to Understanding and Healing.* Lexington, Mass.: Lexington Books, 1987.

Masson, Jeffrey Moussaieff. *The Assault on Truth: Freud's Suppression of the Seduction Theory.* New York: Farrar, Straus, & Giroux, 1984.

McNaran, Toni, and Yarrow Morgan, eds. *Voices in the Night: Women Speaking About Incest.* Minneapolis: Cleis Press, 1982.

Morris, Michelle. *If I Should Die Before I Wake*. New York: Dell, 1982.

Rush, Florence. *The Best-Kept Secret: Sexual Abuse of Children*. Englewood Cliffs, N.J.: Prentice-Hall, 1980.

Russell, Diana. *The Secret Trauma: Incest in the Lives of Girls and Women*. New York: Basic Books, 1986.

OTHER RELEVANT BOOKS

Becnel Cottman, Barbara. *The Co-Dependent Parent: Free Yourself by Freeing Your Child*. Los Angeles: Lowell House, 1990.

Black, Claudia. *Children of Alcoholics: As Youngsters–Adolescents–Adults*. New York: Ballantine Books, 1981.

Bloomfield, Harold, M.D. *Making Peace with Your Parents: The Key to Enriching Your Life and All Your Relationships*. New York: Ballantine Books, 1985.

Bradshaw, John. *Bradshaw On: The Family*. Deerfield Beach, Florida: Health Communications, Inc., 1988.

—— *Healing the Shame That Binds You*. Pompano Beach, Florida: Health Communications, Inc., 1988.

Covitz, Joel. *Emotional Child Abuse: The Family Curse*. Boston: Sigo Press, 1986.

Farmer, Steven. *Adult Children of Abusive Parents*. Los Angeles: Lowell House, 1989.

Forward, Dr. Susan, with Craig Buck. *Toxic Parents: Overcoming Their Hurtful Legacy and Reclaiming Your Life*. New York: Bantam Books, 1989.

Fossum, Merle A., and Marilyn J. Mason. *Facing Shame: Families in Recovery*. New York: W W Norton, 1986.

Halpern, Howard M. *Cutting Loose: An Adult Guide to Coming to Terms with Your Parents*. New York: Bantam Books, 1978.

Miller, Alice. *The Drama of the Gifted Child: The Search for the True Self*. New York: Basic Books, 1981.

—— *Prisoners of Childhood*. New York: Basic Books, 1981.

McDermott, Patti. *Sisters and Brothers*. Los Angeles: Lowell House, 1994.

—— *For Your Own Good: Hidden Cruelty in Child Rearing and the Roots of Violence*. New York: Farrar, Straus & Giroux, 1983.

Resources (Organizations)

Parents United
(Daughters United/Sons United)
P.O. Box 952
San Jose, CA 95108
(408) 280-5055
(408) 279-8228 (crisis line)

A nationwide support organization for incestuous families. Provides weekly professional counseling, lay therapy
groups, and long-term support where incest has been a
factor in family difficulty.

Adults Molested As Children United
P.O. Box 952
San Jose, CA 95108
(408) 280-5055

AMACU is part of Parents United. There are wide differences among individual chapters, so be sure to investigate carefully to make sure that your needs are met. Some
chapters stress forgiveness and family unity as primary
goals, not providing survivors with sufficient support in
expressing their anger or confronting perpetrators. Some
survivors have reported that certain chapters fail to provide adequately trained leaders, maintain appropriate
boundaries between counselors and clients, and/or show
evidence of homophobia. Other survivors have found the

program beneficial because it offers the opportunity to directly confront and work with the perpetrators.

VOICES in Action
P.O. Box 148309
Chicago, IL 60614
(312) 327-1500

International organization for survivors and their partners (prosurvivors).

Parents Anonymous
22330 Hawthorne Blvd., Suite 208
Torrance, CA 90505
(800) 352-0386 (24-hour hotline, California)
(800) 421-0353 (USA, outside California)

This organization has a national hotline and local self-help groups throughout the country for abusive and potentially abusive parents.

Al-Anon Family Group Headquarters
1372 Broadway
New York, NY 10018
(212) 302-7240

Al-Anon provides support services for people related to alcoholics or who have friends with alcohol problems. Alateen, connected to Al-Anon, is a support group for young people aged 12–20 with drinking problems.

Alcoholics Anonymous World Services
P.O. Box 459, Grand Central Station
New York, NY 10163
(212) 686-1100

Alcoholics Anonymous meetings provide a safe place to discuss your problems and gain support and encouragement from others who, like you, have problems with alcohol. All programs are anonymous.

Co-Dependents Anonymous, Inc.
P.O. Box 33577
Phoenix, AZ 85067-3577
(602) 277-7991

This international organization is for people 16 years old and over whose common problem is an inability to maintain functional, healthy relationships with their mates, their children, other family members, friends and co-workers. CODA is a 12-step program.

Families Anonymous
P.O. Box 528
Van Nuys, CA 91408
(800) 736-9805 (24-hour information line)
(818) 989-7841

A self-help program for families and friends of drug abusers, similar to AA (no dues or fees, personal anonymity is preserved).

National Association for Children of Dysfunctional Families
842 Forest Circle
Fond du Lac, WI 54935
(414) 921-6991

Primarily a referral agency to help adult children of dysfunctional families reduce shame, guilt and compulsive behavior. Provides resources and information about support groups in locations nationwide.